GW00419767

Essentials
for every day

PAT GOOCH

TEACHER
TIMESAVERS

Published by Scholastic Publications Ltd,
Villiers House,
Clarendon Avenue,
Leamington Spa,
Warwickshire CV32 5PR

© 1992 Scholastic Publications Ltd

Reprinted 1993, 1993

Author Pat Gooch
Editor Margot O'Keeffe
Sub-editor Jo Saxelby
Series designer Joy White
Designers Joy White and Anna Oliwa
Illustrations Janice Bowles
Animal templates, maps and flags Jo Saxelby
Cover illustration Frances Lloyd
Cover photograph Martyn Chillmaid

Designed using Aldus Pagemaker
Processed by Pages Bureau, Leamington Spa
Artwork by David Harban Design, Warwick
Printed in Great Britain by Clays Ltd, St Ives plc

British Library Cataloguing-in-Publication Data
A catalogue record for this book is
available from the British Library.

ISBN 0-590-53004-6

Contents

This book is designed to save teachers' time. It includes many of the things teachers have spent hours designing or wishing they had time to design. The pages are divided into two main sections: 'General management' and 'Classroom use'.

Some pages can be photocopied straight away and used as they stand. Others need elements to be added to a first photocopy before being copied en masse. For example, on page 42 all you need to do is add the relevant date and type of party before photocopying and sending the sheet home. This particular page can be used on numerous occasions by varying the information added.

General management

This section contains sheets to help with planning, organisation and record keeping as well as letters home to parents, notices and awards for hard work.

Planning

Page 11 is a calendar grid and can be used by the children or the teacher by adding the dates and the month. If required, the grid can be enlarged on the photocopier. Alternatively, this page can be used with pages 112, 113 or 114.

Page 12 is a timetable which can be used in a variety of ways. It has applications for both individuals and groups and could be used by the whole staff to schedule hall times, sports periods, music lessons, rehearsals and so on.

Page 13 is a topic web which can be used in the initial stages of planning a school or class topic.

Page 14 is an annual topic planning sheet which can be used to show all the topics to be followed

over the coming year. This will help with the organisation of communal resources. Each teacher could have a copy so they know, for example, where relevant library books and materials are likely to be at any moment in the term. The sheet divides up into half terms or terms as preferred.

Page 15 is a termly topic sheet and should be used to record a detailed look at a topic which outlines areas to be covered within it.

Page 16 is an assembly rota for planning who is to take each assembly and what theme is to be undertaken. This could be used with the previous sheets (pages 13, 14 and 15) to link class topics with assemblies.

Page 17 is to give a supply teacher useful information on work to be covered, the names of class helpers, those children who need special attention, television programmes to be watched with follow-up work plus which children should be kept apart or watched. The times of breaks and lunch can also be detailed. All supply teachers will be very grateful for the information.

Planning					
Daily group tasks					
PANTHERS		LEOPARDS		CHEETAHS	
1 MATHS Bk2 pp29-31		1 ENGLISH POEM 'Smugglers'		1 SCIENCE INVESTIGATION	
2 ENGLISH POEM 'Smugglers'		2 SCIENCE INESTIGATION		2 ART COLLAGE	
3 SCIENCE INVESTIGATION		3 ART COLLAGE		3 PROJECT 'SPACE'	
4 ART COLLAGE		4 PROJECT 'SPACE'		4 MATHS BK1 pp35-36	
5 PROJECT 'SPACE'		5 MATHS Bk2 pp 29-31		5 ENGLISH BOOK AE p6	
LIONS		TIGERS		WOLVES	
1 PROJECT 'SPACE'		1 MATHS PRACTICAL		1 ENGLISH WORKBOOK p3	
2 MATHS WORKCARDS 59		2 ENGLISH WORKBOOK p5+6		2 MATHS PRACTICAL	
3 ENGLISH COMPREHENSION WORKSHEET		3 ART FREE CHOICE		3 PROJECT 'SPACE'	
4 SCIENCE INVESTIGATION		4 PROJECT 'SPACE'		4 SCIENCE INVESTIGATION	
5 ART FREE CHOICE		5 SCIENCE INVESTIGATION		5 ART FREE CHOICE	

18   *Essentials for every day*

This page could be used in conjunction with page 12 which gives the times of regular activities such as games or music lessons.

Page 18 provides a framework for linking daily group tasks. Fill in the work to be covered by the groups in your class along with times if necessary. Pin it up where it is accessible to all the children, who can refer to it instead of asking you what to do next. Keep the sheet afterwards as a record of the work covered by each group during the day.

Organisation

Page 19 is to be used as a record of all aspects of a trip, from who to contact through to a record of costs. Anyone could pick this up and organise the trip if required. The last section should be used as a record of the success, or otherwise, of the trip and to outline improvements which could be made next time.

Pages 20-21 can be used to list what needs to be recorded from the television or radio and also to check that it has been done. The list should be updated when programmes change.

Page 22 will help to avoid arguments over the use of communal resources, as those who book required items using this form will have priority. The sheet will also serve as a record of when people had the equipment and whether they returned it.

Page 23 provides a useful record of planned staff absences and their class requirements. If work is set, it should be recorded here. If a member of staff is following a series of courses, this sheet could be used to plan having the same supply or cover teacher throughout, giving the class continuity.

Page 24 should be used to list all the supply teachers you have found particularly reliable, with their specialisms, to provide an immediately accessible resource.

Page 25 can be used to list the parent helpers in the school, their strengths or interests and the classes they assist. This could also be used by individual teachers to list the parents who help with their class. It would be a useful record for supply teachers or the teacher taking the class the following year.

Page 26 is for listing classroom helpers and their jobs. It will be particularly valuable to supply teachers and will encourage children to be helpful and organise themselves. It will need to be changed on a regular basis.

Records

Page 27 encourages children to read a variety of books. The sheet can be used on a monthly or termly basis. Each category could be illustrated as a book is read, or the children could write titles and authors.

Page 28 should be filled in by the children as a book report. Keep the reports in a file in the book corner as recommended reading suggestions. Ask the children to decorate the outside of the file to make it as inviting as possible.

Page 29 is for comments on books, for the children to keep a record of what they have read. It can be filled in either by the children or teacher. Put enough sheets in a file for each child to have one. As the child finishes his book, so he fills in this sheet showing what he has read. This is ideal as a record of books read.

Page 30 is a shared reading record and should be completed by the adult or partner as required. Keep the sheets in a folder for the group to fill in or to be sent home with the home reading book for the parent or adult to complete.

Page 31 is an all-purpose evaluation sheet for a class or group. It is intended as a group record rather than an individual one and might be used, for example, to evaluate a group's problem-solving or drama activities.

Pages 32-37 are simple record sheets for attainment targets in maths, English, science, technology, history and geography. The Key has been left open so that the system adopted by the school can be used here. Fill in the school's own rating system as required.

Page 38 is a general record sheet for adapting to a number of uses, including children's own records of achievement.

Page 39 is a supply teacher's report form intended to encourage the supply teacher to leave details of work covered for the class teacher. S/he should also be encouraged to give details on this sheet of helpful children and problems which have occurred.

Page 40 is for use with all children who have to take medication. Have two copies; the first will be of children with long-term medication needs, such as diabetes and asthma, while the second will be for short-term medication. Anyone should be able to take over this duty easily. It can also be used as a record that medication has been given when due and by whom.

Page 41 is a record of an individual child's medication giving details of dosage and frequency. This page should be used alongside page 40.

Records
Shared reading record

Names	GREGORY SHEPHERD, GRAHAM MARTINS, JOHN GORMAN	
Date	Book	Comment
15·9·91 17·9·91 18·9·91	The Witches ROALD DAHL Finished	All the boys thoroughly enjoyed the humour in this book and want to read more by the same author.

30 | Essentials for every day

Records
English

English — Name *Jenny Russell*, Class *R*

Level	AT1	AT2	AT3	AT4	AT5	KEY
1	◯		⊙		◯	
2						Covered
3						⊙
4						Needs work
5						☺
6						Understood and remembered

Essentials for every day | 33

Records
Medication - Individual

Name:	FRED SIMPSON		Amount:	2 PUFFS EACH	
Medications:	VENTOLIN + BECOTIDE		Times:	12.30 p.m. 3.30 p.m.	
Date	Times	Signed	Date	Times	Signed
5·9·91	12·30p.m. ✓ 3·30p.m. ✓	PKS. PKS.	12·9·91	OFF SICK	
6·9·91	12·30p.m. ✓ 3·30p.m. ✓	PKS. R.J.	13·9·91		
7·9·91	12·30p.m. ✓ 3·30p.m. ✓	PKS. PKS.	14·9·91		
8·8·91	12·30p.m. 3·30p.m.	MJT MJT	15·9·91	12·30p.m. 3·30p.m.	PKS. PKS.
9·9·91	12·30p.m. 3·30p.m.	R.J. R.J.	16·9·91	12·30p.m. 3·30p.m.	R.J. R.J.

Essentials for every day | 41

Letters, notices and awards

Page 42 can be used on numerous occasions by filling in the details of the type of party and the date. It can also be used as a record of what each child is supposed to be providing for the party, ensuring that not everyone brings crisps!

Page 43 is a class trip letter requiring the details of the trip to be entered plus the date. The reply slip will act both as a permission slip and a record of money received.

Page 44 is a letter asking for junk material. Send this letter out on a regular basis to ensure that each class has all the items it needs.

Page 45 informs parents and guardians of the part their child has been given in a school performance. Fill in the correct details in the spaces provided on the first photocopy before duplicating the required number. It can also be a request for help with costumes: The reply slip is a record that the parent has seen the letter.

Page 46 is a letter to ask for help with any activity going on in school, including the school play. The letter has been kept very open. Fill in the details of what event is planned and what help is needed. This might range from helping with sponsored activities to cleaning out the school swimming pool.

Page 47 is one that most teachers have had to send out at some time. The aim is to explain to parents and guardians that head lice are not unusual or something of which to be ashamed. Send this letter out every time an outbreak occurs to try to control it before it spreads too far.

Page 48 is a general illness letter which will inform parents and guardians of the outbreak of any common childhood illness which their child might catch. Parents will be grateful for the advice on incubation periods and how long to keep their child at home, as well as information

on the symptoms. For many parents it will be the first time they come across this illness.

Page 49 can be used either as a poster or as a letter, depending on the information you add to the first photocopy. It can emphasise to the parent the other aspects of an open evening besides going to see the class teacher. It is designed to show that the school extends a warm welcome to parents.

Page 50 is an open evening appointments notice to show parents and guardians the times of their appointments. It can be pinned up as reference for all those waiting. The children could help to decorate it.

Page 51, like page 49, can either be used as a poster or as a letter depending on the way the information is added to the page. The children can decorate the page and it can then be used to advertise the event.

Page 52 is a sports day notice which can be used as a poster or letter to inform parents and guardians of the time and date of the event. Later, the individual events can be listed on another copy and it will become a programme of events. Let the children decorate a copy, including the details of the day and time, and it becomes an advertisement which can be placed in windows around the location (with permission, of course) to encourage the community to join in the event.

Page 53 is a sports results notice - a record of all the winners of each event which will help with scores at the end of the day. Whether you call the positions first, second and third or gold, silver and bronze is up to you.

Page 54 provides an opportunity to advertise the fact that your school is having a book week. Use it to list all the events that will happen during the book week as well as to encourage parents to come to those events which are applicable. Send it out first as an advance warning of the event giving the date, time and outline. Use it nearer the time to list in detail the events with dates and times. Copies can be decorated and used as posters in school.

Page 55 is a school performance notice to be used as a poster to advertise the event. It can be used for the school play, for a concert or any other performance put on by the school.

Page 56 should be used to notify parents and guardians of their child's involvement in the school performance and the commitment expected. The list of rehearsals means the cast know in advance who is needed when so that they can plan accordingly.

Page 57 is a props request to staff, children, friends of the school and local shops for props which are required for the school performance.

It is also a check that items that were borrowed are returned from whence they came.

Page 58, like page 57, can also be used as a check that whatever is borrowed is returned as soon as the play is over.

Page 59 is intended as a reward for a struggling reader who has tried particularly hard. The child is measured against himself, not his peers.

Page 60 aims to encourage parents and guardians to share in the development of their child's reading, through reading together in the evening.

Page 61 is an award which, similar to page 59, is for a child who is struggling with maths and has made a personal achievement.

Page 62 has the same aims as the previous three pages. These pages must be used with care as a spur to motivate those who need the morale boost. They must not be given lightly.

Classroom use

This section includes material which can be used by individual children or whole groups. It includes activities for reinforcing skills plus attractively illustrated pages for display and celebrations.

The basics

Pages 63-67 can be used in a variety of ways, including as headings for display boards, titles on large classroom-made books or as part of a frieze. Sizes can be varied on the photocopier.

Pages 68-70 can be used in a variety of ways, from helping to teach children how to read and write music to preparing individual parts for the school orchestra or choir.

Page 71 is for telling the time on an analogue clock. The clock face blanks can be used for whatever stage the child is at, from o'clock to '55 minutes past'. Either draw in the hands and the child writes the time or vice-versa.

Page 72 is to be used to teach the time using a digital clock face. Either write the time in words while the child writes the time on the digital face or vice-versa. It can also be used to teach the 24-hour clock.

Pages 73-78 are the flags of the United Kingdom, the Republic of Ireland and the Isle of Man.

Page 79 represents the EC flag which will be unfamiliar to many children or teachers. Use it as the stimulus to some interesting research on the structure of the flag itself.

Pages 80-86 are maps of the UK as parts and as a whole, Europe and the world. They can be used for a variety of purposes.

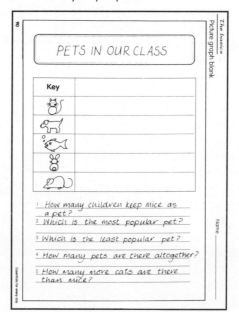

Page 87 has two simple crossword blanks which can be used to introduce how crosswords work. The first just has words going across and the second progresses on to words going across and down. By drawing a frame around the second crossword it can be made more complicated and more like a conventional crossword grid.

Page 88 is a conventional crossword grid on which the children can work out their own puzzles and try them on each other.

Page 89 is a wordsearch grid which can also be used as a complicated crossword grid or a number square.

Page 90 is a picture graph. It needs the symbols for the key to be drawn in depending on what you want the graph to be about. For example, for a graph of the favourite pets in the class draw symbols for dogs, cats, rabbits and fish in the key. Make the pictures very simple to copy and give instructions at the top. In the spaces provided, write questions for the children to answer using the graph.

Page 91 is a bar graph. Again, there are spaces for instructions and questions. This page can be used on numerous occasions with children of different abilities merely by varying the instructions and the questions.

Page 92 is a line graph with spaces for instructions or for questions underneath. These graphs can be used time and time again for different activities.

Display

Page 93 enables each child to have their own clock face with moveable hands. Mount it on card and then cut it out. The hands can be attached to the face with a brass fastener. This page could be used with pages 71 and 72.

Title *Charlie and the Chocolate Factory*
Author *Roald Dahl*

Favourite character *Willie Wonka*

Best part of the book *At the end in the elevator*

Pages 94-95 will help to build up a bookworm for your wall display. Put up page 94 as the head. The children fill in a copy of page 95 every time they read a really good book. The segments are intended as book reviews telling the rest of the class about books which the children recommend as an enjoyable read. The display can be changed every few weeks. Do not throw away the finished segments. Put them in a file in the book corner for reference.

Pages 96-100 are outlines of dinosaurs, birds, reptiles, sea creatures and mammals which can be used in a variety of ways, from colouring to work on sets. They could also be used to decorate worksheets or books the children have made themselves. The creatures represented on each page are as follows (clockwise from top left-hand corner):
Page 96 - stegosaurus, diplodocus, pteranodon, tyrannosaurus rex, triceratops.
Page 97 - kingfisher, robin, cockerel, kestrel, mute swan.
Page 98 - crocodile, chameleon, terrapin, tuatara, snake.

Page 99 - sea horse, jelly fish, shark, octopus, butterfly fish, pike, ray.
Page 100 - rhesus monkey, dolphin, elephant, bat, hedgehog, mouse.
Pages 101-102 are for use on a class weather chart. There are nine weather categories which can be simplified if required. Enlarge if necessary on the photocopier.
Pages 103-109 can be used for creative or factual writing related to the religion or festival represented. These sheets could also be used to make cards to celebrate feast days.
Pages 110-111 provide attractive borders for creative writing on the themes of bonfire night and space.
Pages 112-114 give the months of the year to be used on a seasonal wall display or in conjunction with page 11, 101 and 102.

Special occasions

Page 115 needs the correct number of candles added to celebrate a child's birthday. Write the child's name and age in the spaces provided. It can then be decorated as required.

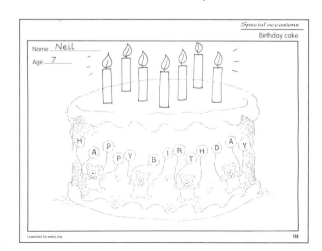

Special occasions
Birthday cake

Name *Neil*
Age *7*

HAPPY BIRTHDAY

Essentials for every day   115

Pages 116-119 can be used for individual activities. Decorate them as required, add any rhymes or verses and fold as instructed to form into cards which will stand up by themselves. The children will also be able to use these sheets as templates to make their own cards.

All about me

Page 120 will be invaluable to supply teachers at any time and class teachers at the beginning of each new year. When folded this page makes a free-standing name badge.
Page 121 asks for information about the children and what they feel about themselves. Sensitivity needs to be shown when asking for this kind of personal response. If a child does not want to fill in any section do not insist that they do.
Pages 122-123 provide alternative outlines to stimulate diary writing. They could be used to build up a long-term diary with the cover designed and made by the child.
Page 124 calls for a personal assessment by the children. Ask them to fill it in at different points in the year and compare it with previous assessments to see their progress.
Page 125 is for fun. Emphasise that the fingerprints will not be kept by the school - some families may be very sensitive on this subject. Use the sheet to show that we are all different and to challenge the children to discover the different patterns and swirls.
Page 126 must be used with sensitivity. When discussing the concept of family trees, emphasise that the device can be used for immediate family whether related or not.
Page 127 looks at the history of names and where they come from, which all children find fascinating. The children could make up names for the characters on the illustration.

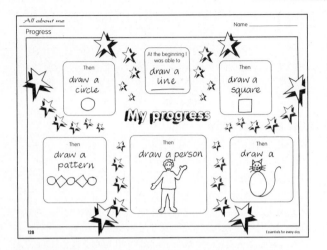

Page 128 provides an opportunity for children to assess their own progress in relation to their development and not on comparative or competitive terms. Ask them to draw arrows indicating the direction of their progress.

Page 129 requires the children to guess how long it takes them to do routine activities and then to actually time them to see how good their guess was. At the same time, it encourages them to complete the activities on a regular basis.

Page 130 encourages the children to get into the habit of being clean and tidy. How many of them do not see all the items on this page as a regular part of their daily routine? Use this sheet to encourage discussion on health and caring for their bodies.

Page 131 asks the children to find out which illnesses and which injections they have had. Discussions should follow on the reasons for injections and preventive medicine.

Page 132 looks at all aspects of the child's size, from his height and weight to the size of his smile. Use this sheet sensitively.

Anytime activities

Page 133 is an activity the children will want to do time and time again. Insert some first names from your class in code. The children have to encode the surnames and write them down. Write in code the names of relevant famous people and animals in the correct boxes for the children to decode. Some have been done for you already.

The code A + 2 is:
A B C D E F G H   and so on
3 4 5 6 7 8 9 10

The code A = 6 is:
A B C D E F G H   and so on
6 7 8 9 10 11 12 13

The third code is simply:
A B C D E F G H   and so on
B C D E F G H I

Encourage the children to make up their own codes and try them out on their friends.

Page 134 is a 'snakes and ladders' word puzzle page for the children to try. Fill in the first and last word on the word ladder. The children have to change one letter on each rung of the ladder to get from the first to the last word in the correct number of rungs, for example, test - tent - rent - rant - pant - pane or road - roar - boar - bear - beat - bent - sent - seat. Let the children make up their own versions.

Page 135 will encourage the children to become familiar with their school dictionary. Choose a page from the dictionary and write it in the space provided. Then choose words from that page of the dictionary which fit each of the spaces on the sheet. This sheet can be used many times by varying the page and the words you choose and can be used with all abilities by careful choice of the words and pages.

Page 136 needs a picture of what you want the children to describe. They then find four words for each section to describe that picture. Make sure the picture will photocopy. Keep it simple and bold.

Page 137 also needs pictures in each of the boxes of the items you want the children to describe and the adjective you want changed to be written in. Two have been done for you.

Page 138 can be used for a variety of activities to develop the concept of sets. For example, draw in eight shapes of which only some are round. Photocopy the sheet and ask the children to colour all the round items in red. Eventually you could ask the children to draw the set themselves. At a more advanced level, you could write in two or three word families and ask the children to subset the words.

Page 139 is a starting point for research and further activity. The children will use this page to work from, not on. Nothing needs to be added before the page is photocopied and given to the child or group. It is intended as a group activity, but it can be used on an individual basis.

Page 140 provides an opportunity for children to practise measurement skills. It can be adapted to your classroom environment. Fill in items available in your classroom for the objects the children are to measure. Make it more difficult by putting in a few 'red herrings'!

Page 141, like page 139, is a stimulus for further activity. The children will work from this sheet not on it, preferably in small groups or pairs.

Pages 142-144 provide useful nets of basic geometric models. Enlarge or reduce them on the photocopier as required.

Essentials for every day

Topic planning - termly

Topic	Class	Term

Language

Science

Maths

RE

History

Technology

Art

Geography

Dance, drama and PE

Music

Assembly rota

Day	Date	Class	Teacher	Subject/theme

Notes to supply teacher

Language	Maths	Science	Other	Watch out for!

TV or Radio programmes

Break-times

Morning

Lunch

Afternoon

Helpers

Daily group tasks

1 2 3 4 5	1 2 3 4 5	1 2 3 4 5
1 2 3 4 5	1 2 3 4 5	1 2 3 4 5

School outing to _____

Date of outing	Contacts	
Teacher(s)	Classes	Total children
Educational rationale		
Bus company	Tel:	Number of buses
Cost per bus	Deposit required Yes/No	Paid Yes/No
Total cost	Cost per child	Difference
Parents required Yes/No	Number per class	
Names		
Depart school	Arrive location	
Depart location	Arrive school	
Full/Half day	Packed lunch required Yes/No	Parents notified Yes/No
Comments on the trip's success		

Term_____

TV timetable

	Programme title	Channel	Day shown	Time	Repeated	Time	Recorded	By

Term_____

Radio timetable

Programme title	Date	Time	Length	Station	Teacher

Essentials for every day

Loan requests

Date	Request	Teacher	Taken	Returned

Staff cover

Teacher absent	Date	Time	Class	Covered by	Work set

Supply teachers

Name	Address	Phone	Specialism	Year preference

Parent helpers

Name	Interests	Day(s) / time available	Class

Helpers and jobs

Helpers	Jobs

Name _____

Animals

Fairy-tale

Sports

Mystery

Books I have read

Non-fiction

Adventure

Other

Science fiction

Essentials for every day

My favourite book

My favourite book

The main characters are

The part in the book I like best

I like this part because

Some more of my favourite books are

My favourite book when I was little was

because

Name _____

Book comments

Book title	Page	Date	Comments

Shared reading record

Names		
Date	**Book**	**Comment**

Class/group	Subject	Evaluation

Mathematics AT record

	Mathematics				Name Class	
Level	AT1	AT2	AT3	AT4	AT5	KEY
1						
2						Covered
3						
4						Needs work
5						
6						Understood and remembered

English

| | | | | | Name |
| | | | | | Class |

Level	AT1	AT2	AT3	AT4	AT5	KEY
1						
2						Covered
3						
4						Needs work
5						
6						Understood and remembered

Science AT record

Level	AT1	AT2	AT3	AT4	KEY
Science			Name / Class		
1					
2					Covered
3					
4					Needs work
5					
6					Understood and remembered

Technology					Name Class	
Level	AT1	AT2	AT3	AT4	AT5	KEY
1						
2						Covered
3						
4						Needs work
5						
6						Understood and remembered

History AT record

Level	AT1	AT2	AT3		KEY
			History	Name	
				Class	
1				CSUs	
2					Covered
3					
4				SSUs	Needs work
5					
6					Understood and remembered

Geography AT record

Level	AT1	AT2	AT3	AT4	AT5	KEY
			Geography		**Name** **Class**	
1						
2						Covered
3						
4						Needs work
5						
6						Understood and remembered

General record sheet

Record sheet

Supply teacher's report

Name _____

Phone _____

Date _____ Class _____

Notes received _____

_____

Particularly helpful children _____

Children needing additional help _____

Reading _____

Mathematics _____

Language _____

Science _____

Other _____

Comments _____

_____

Medication details - general

Child	Class	Medication	Times to be taken

Medication details - individual

Name:			Amount:		
Medications:			Times:		
Date	**Times**	**Signed**	**Date**	**Times**	**Signed**

Party letter

We're having a party!

Dear Parent

We are having a _____ party for our

_____ class on _____

Each child is asked to bring a plate of party food. The plate should be disposable, or plastic and clearly labelled to ensure return.

Your child's contribution has been circled below.

sandwiches   small cakes/slices   nuts/crisps

sweets   sausages   sausage rolls

fruit   drink   other

With thanks

_____
Class teacher

_____
Child's name

_____
Class

Dear Parent

Class(es) _____ is/are going on a school trip

to _____ on _____

The trip will cost £____ per child and any contribution from you would be gratefully received.

We suggest a maximum of £____ spending money is necessary. Please do not be cajoled into giving more.

The children will/will not need a packed lunch. No glass bottles please.

They will leave at _____ from _____

and return at _____

Yours sincerely

--- ✂ ---

Dear _____

I give/do not give permission for _____

to go on the school trip to _____

on _____

Please find enclosed a contribution of £ _____

Signed _____ (Parent/Guardian)

Scrap materials letter

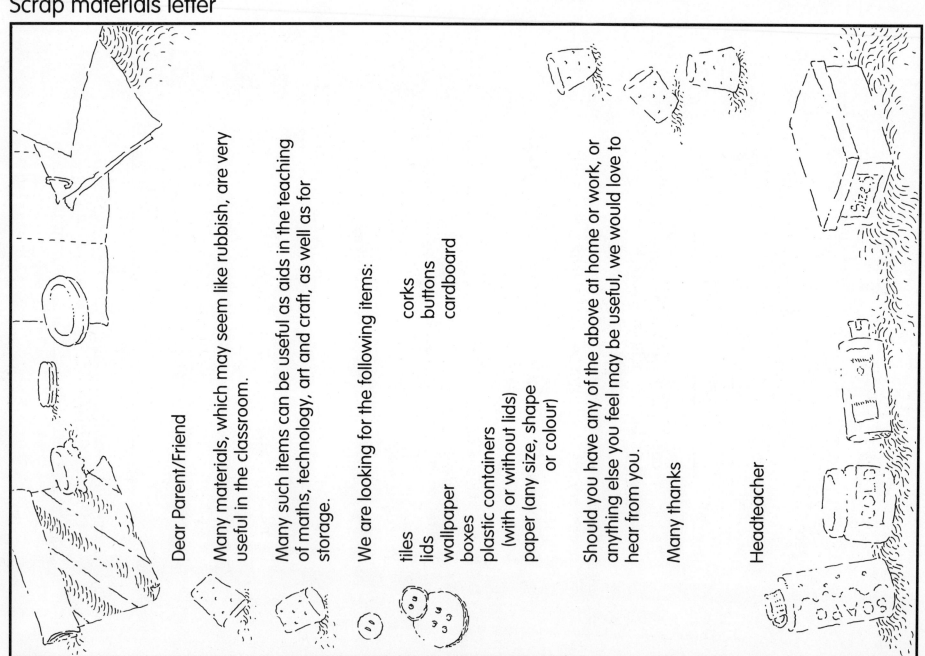

Dear Parent/Friend

Many materials, which may seem like rubbish, are very useful in the classroom.

Many such items can be useful as aids in the teaching of maths, technology, art and craft, as well as for storage.

We are looking for the following items:

tiles
lids
wallpaper
boxes
plastic containers
    (with or without lids)
paper (any size, shape
    or colour)

corks
buttons
cardboard

Should you have any of the above at home or work, or anything else you feel may be useful, we would love to hear from you.

Many thanks

Headteacher

44

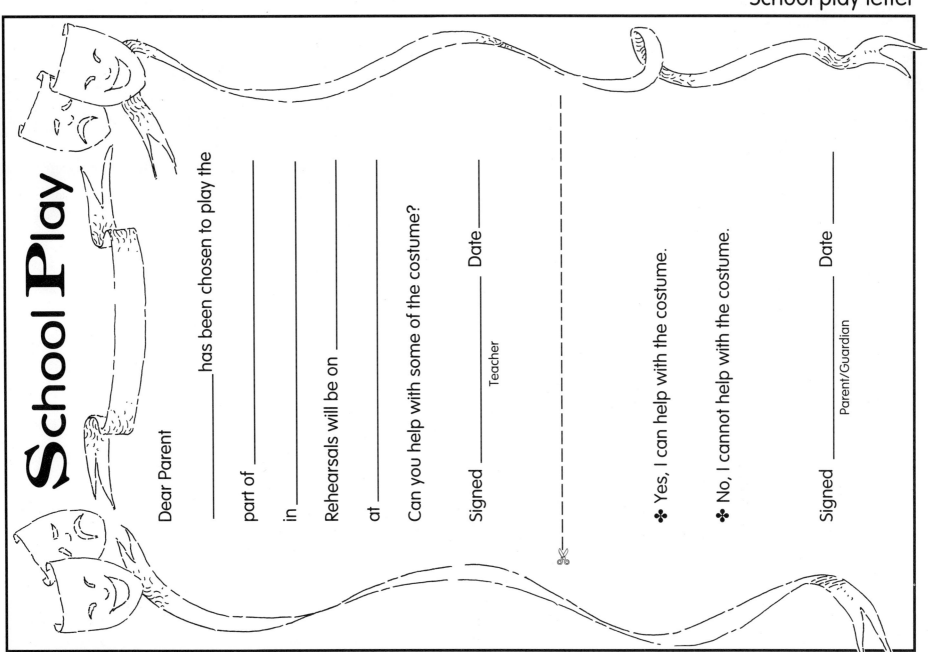

School Play

Dear Parent

_____ has been chosen to play the

part of _____

in _____

Rehearsals will be on _____

at _____

Can you help with some of the costume?

Signed _____ Date _____
            Teacher

- ❖ Yes, I can help with the costume.

- ❖ No, I cannot help with the costume.

Signed _____ Date _____
            Parent/Guardian

Can you help letter

Can you lend a hand

Dear Parent

Our class is planning _____

_____

_____

We need your help with _____

_____

If you can help, please sign and return the slip below.

Many thanks

_____
Class teacher

✂ -

Dear _____

I should like to help Class _____ with _____

Signed _____
Parent/Guardian

Date _____

Head lice letter

❖❖❖❖❖❖❖❖❖❖❖❖❖❖❖❖❖❖❖❖❖❖❖❖❖❖❖❖❖

Dear Parent

A few children have been found to have head lice.
This is a problem that occurs from time to time.

Please help us to get rid of this problem.

❖ Check your child's hair on a regular basis.
❖ As soon as you suspect infection, treat with special shampoo from the chemist. Don't forget that head lice love clean hair, so don't let your child be ashamed.
❖ Inform us of the problem.
❖ Repeat the treatment after six weeks to catch any hatched eggs.
❖ Comb the hair at least twice a day with a fine-tooth comb. This will catch any head lice acquired during that day before they have a chance to lay eggs.

We seek your co-operation in this matter to keep this problem at bay.

Thank you.

Headteacher

❖❖❖❖❖❖❖❖❖❖❖❖❖❖❖❖❖❖❖❖❖❖❖❖❖❖❖❖❖

General illness letter

Dear Parent

I am writing to inform you that we have an outbreak of _____ in the school.

The early symptoms to look for are _____

As soon as you suspect that your child has the early symptoms, keep him or her at home and inform the school.

You must keep your child at home for at least _____ or until _____

Headteacher

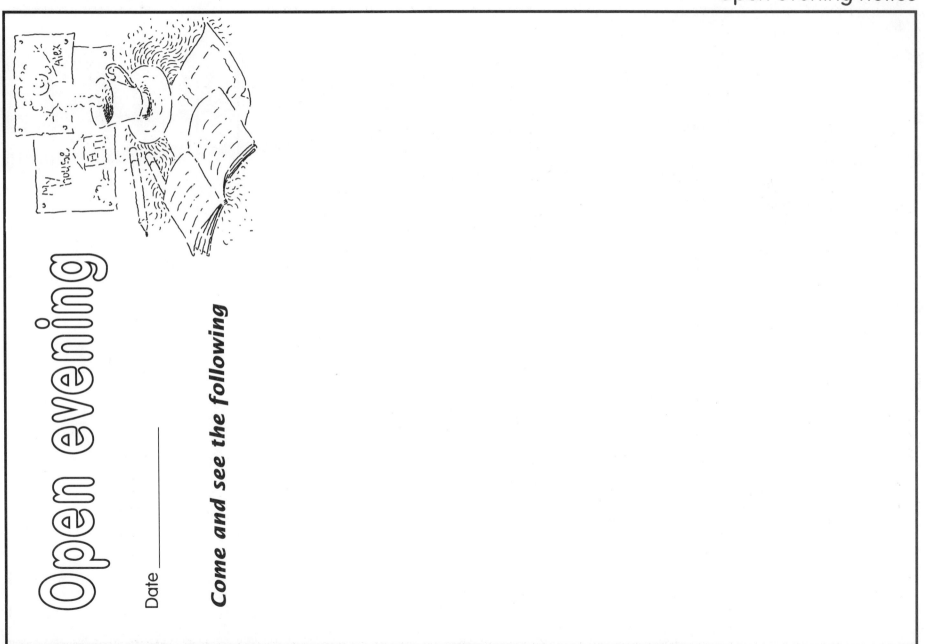

Open evening

Date _____

Come and see the following

Open evening appointments

Open evening

Appointment times

Open day notice

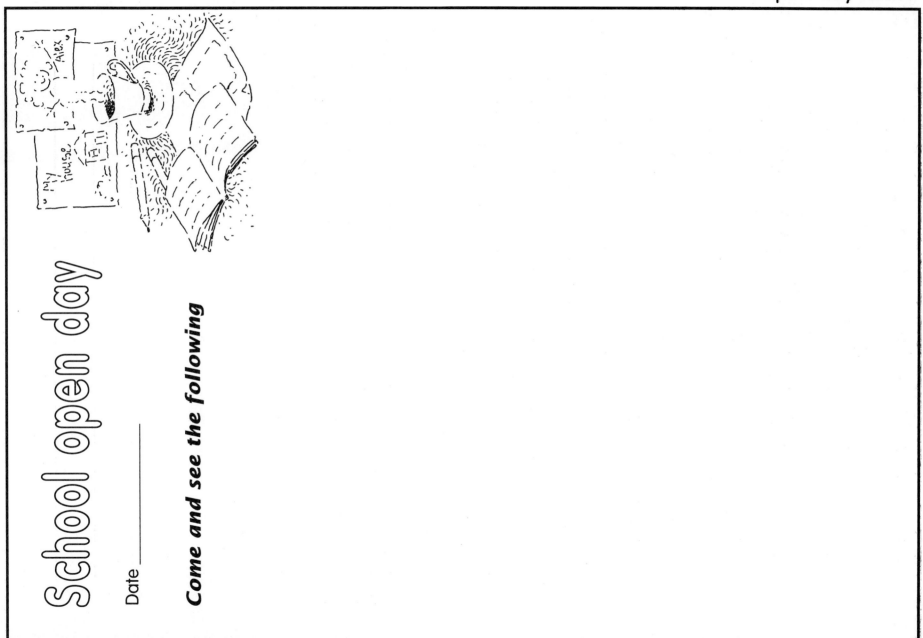

School open day

Date _____

Come and see the following

Sports day notice

School Sports Day

Sports results

Event	Age	Gold (name)	Class/house	Silver (name)	Class/house	Bronze (name)	Class/house

BOOK WEEK

Rehearsal schedule

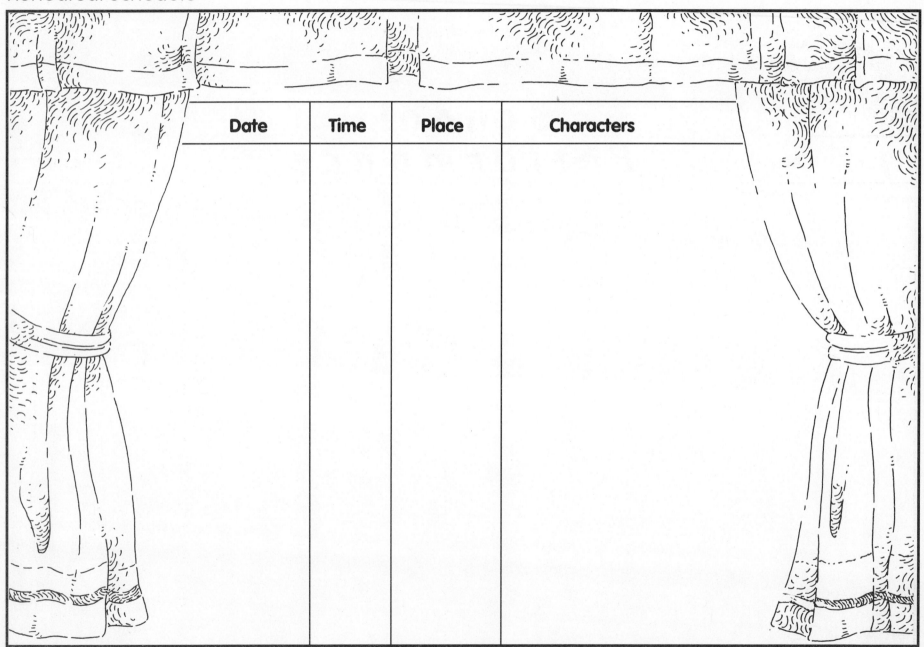

Date	Time	Place	Characters

Props request

**We need the following props.
Can you help?**

Character	Prop	Lent by	Made by	Returned by

Costume request

**We need the following costumes.
Can you help?**

Character	Costume	Size	Lent by	Made by	Returned by

Most Improved Reader Award

Presented to

_____

for progress and achievement in reading

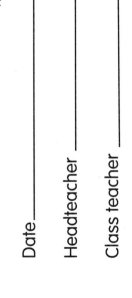

Date _____

Headteacher _____

Class teacher _____

Shared reading certificate

Shared Reading Certificate

Awarded to

*and parent or guardian
for shared reading experiences*

Date

Headteacher

Class teacher

Most improved mathematician

%

Most
Improved
Mathematician

Presented to

*for progress and
achievement in mathematics*

$6 + 2 =$

Date

Headteacher

Class teacher

Most improved scientist

Most Improved Scientist

Presented to

for progress and achievement in science

Date

Headteacher

Class teacher

a b c d e f g

h i j k l m

n o p q r s

Alphabet 2 (lower case)

t u v w x y z

, ; : . ' " ! ? ( )

A B C D E
F G H I J
K L M N

Alphabet 2 (upper case)

O P Q R S
T U V W
X Y Z

0 1 2 3 4 5

6 7 8 9 - +

Treble clef

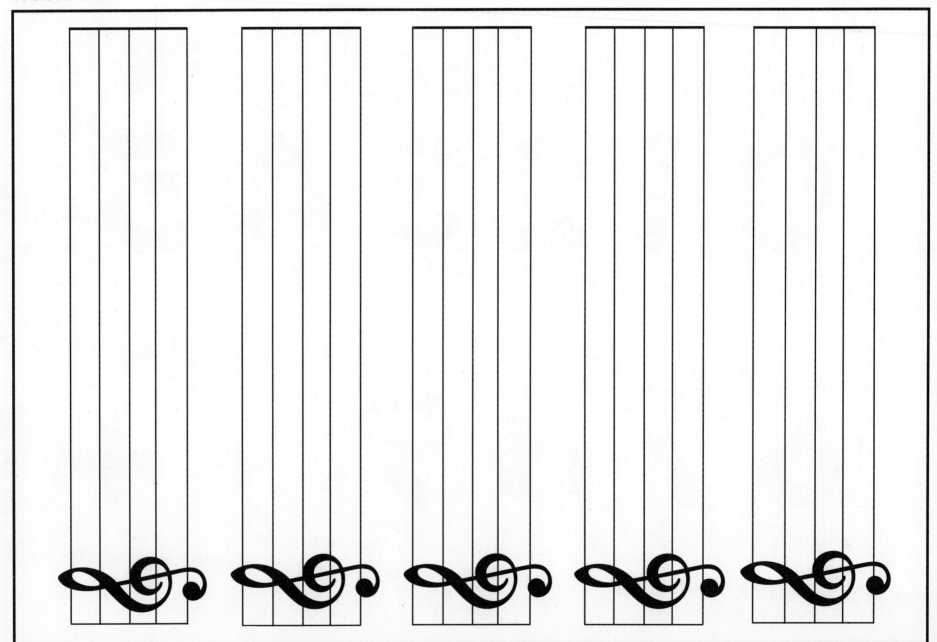

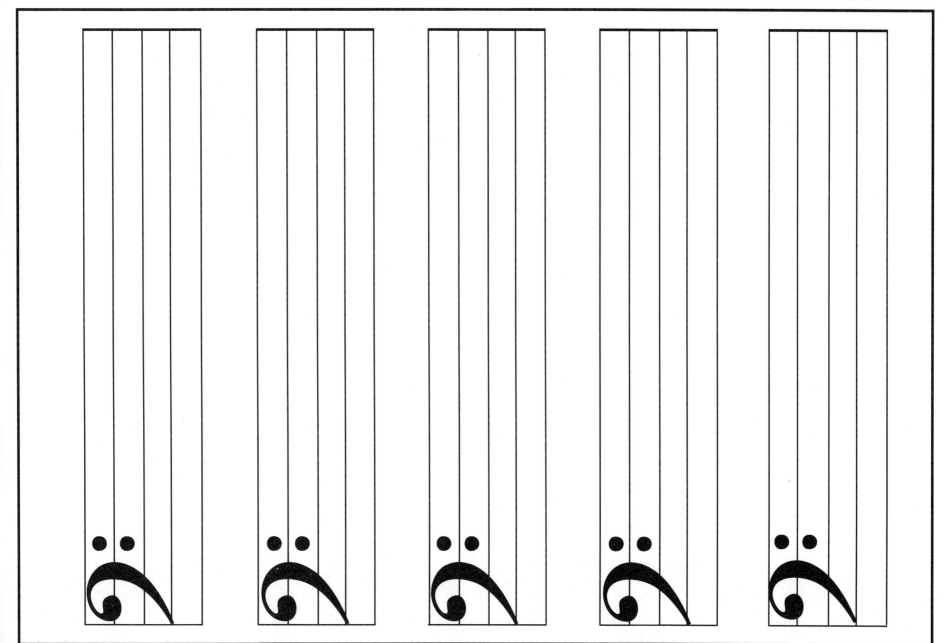

Treble and bass clef

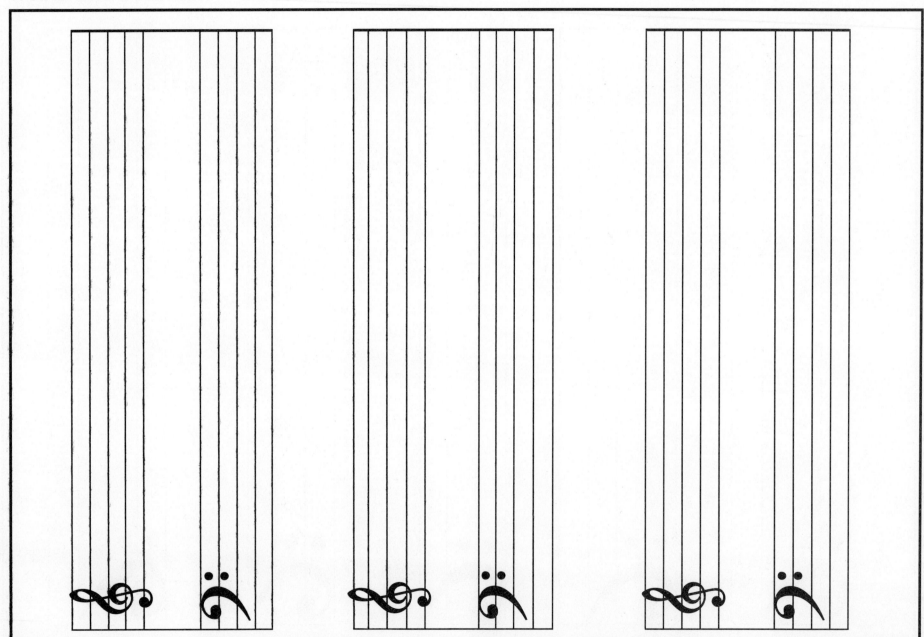

Analogue clock face blanks

_____

_____

_____

_____

_____

_____

Digital clock face blanks

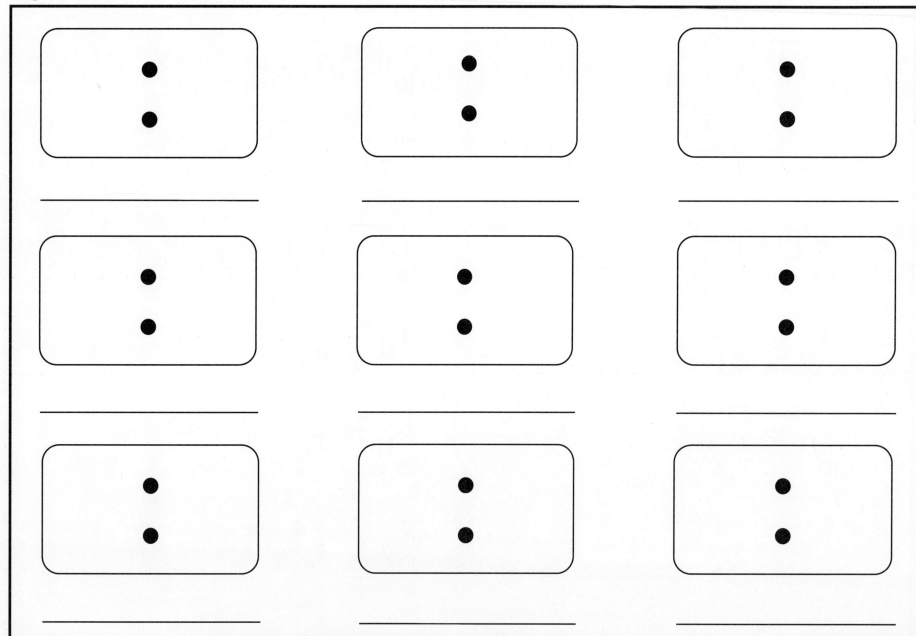

Welsh flag

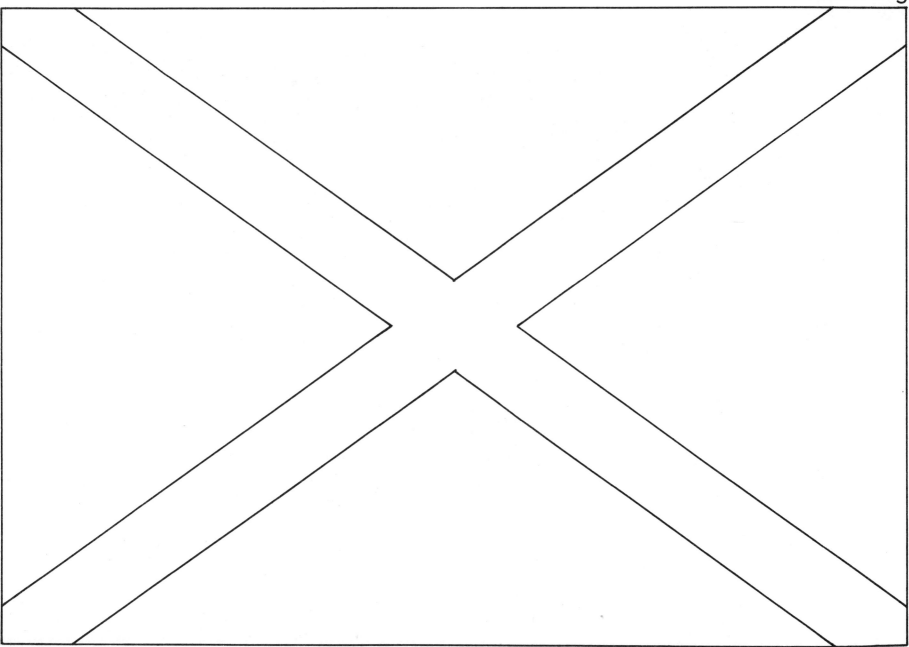

Isle of Man flag

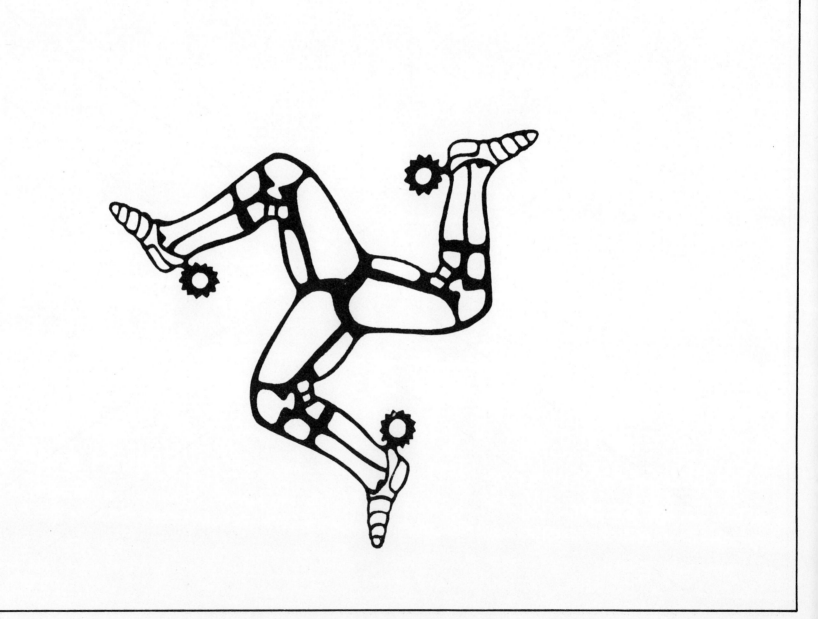

Republic of Ireland flag

Union Jack

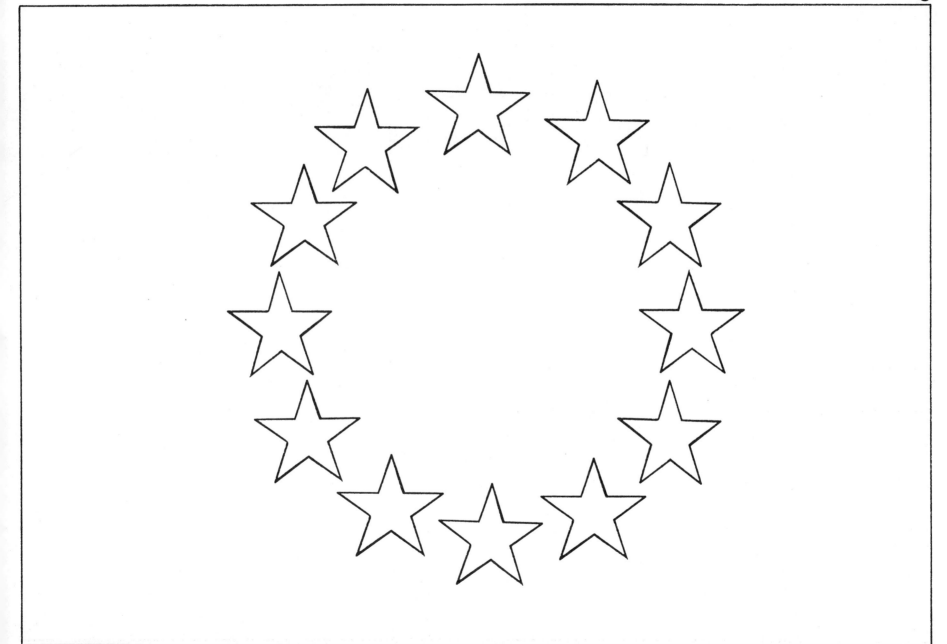

Map of England

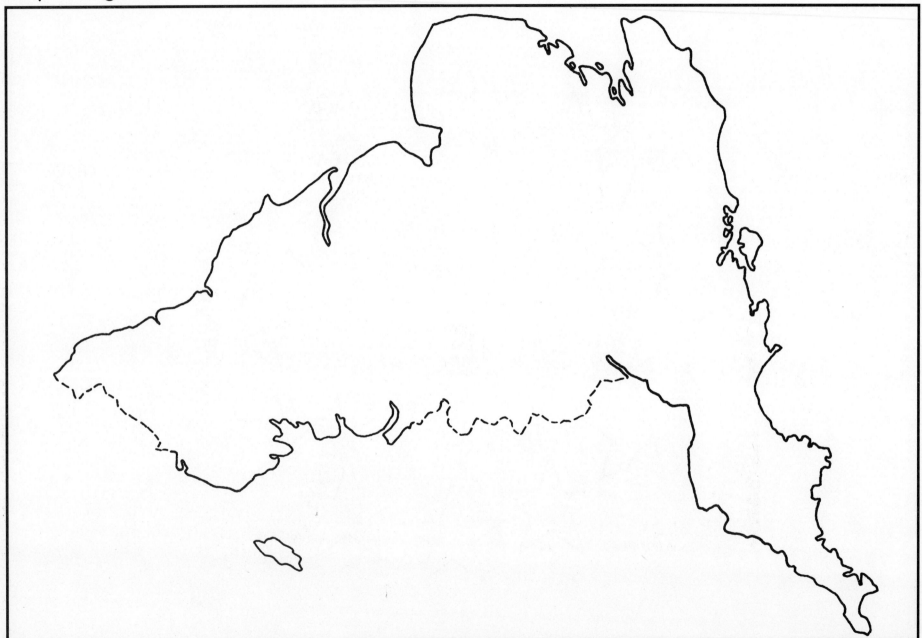

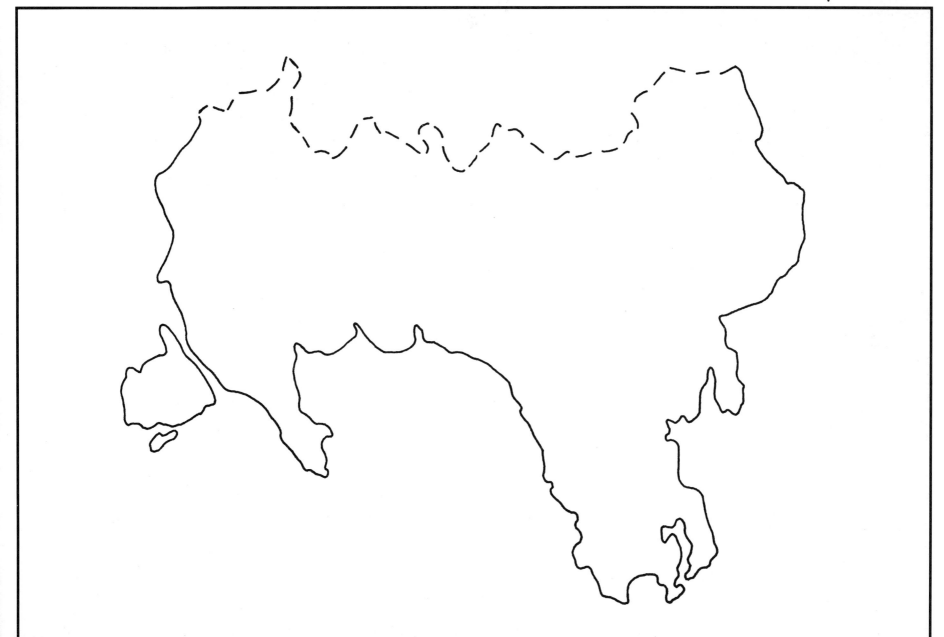

Map of Scotland

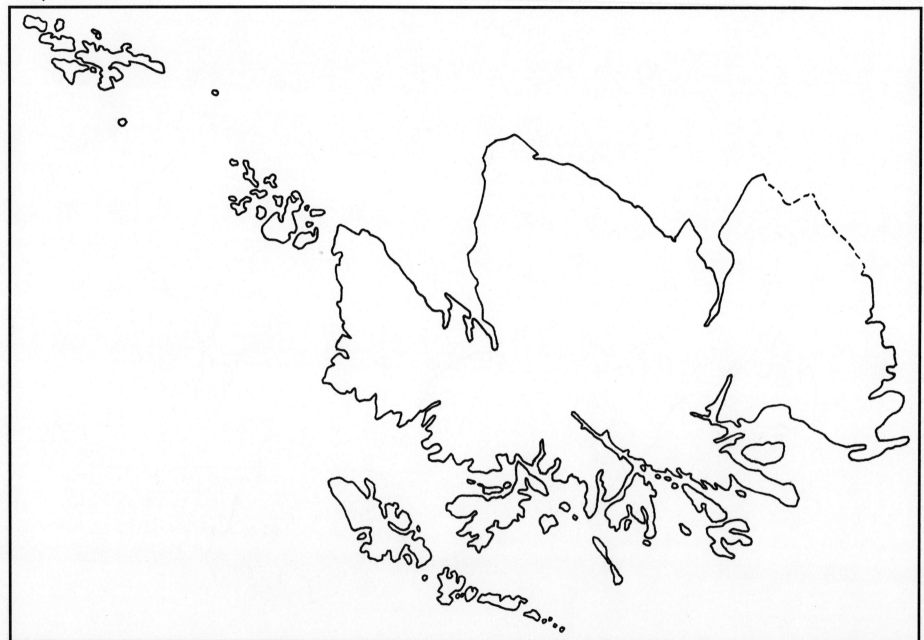

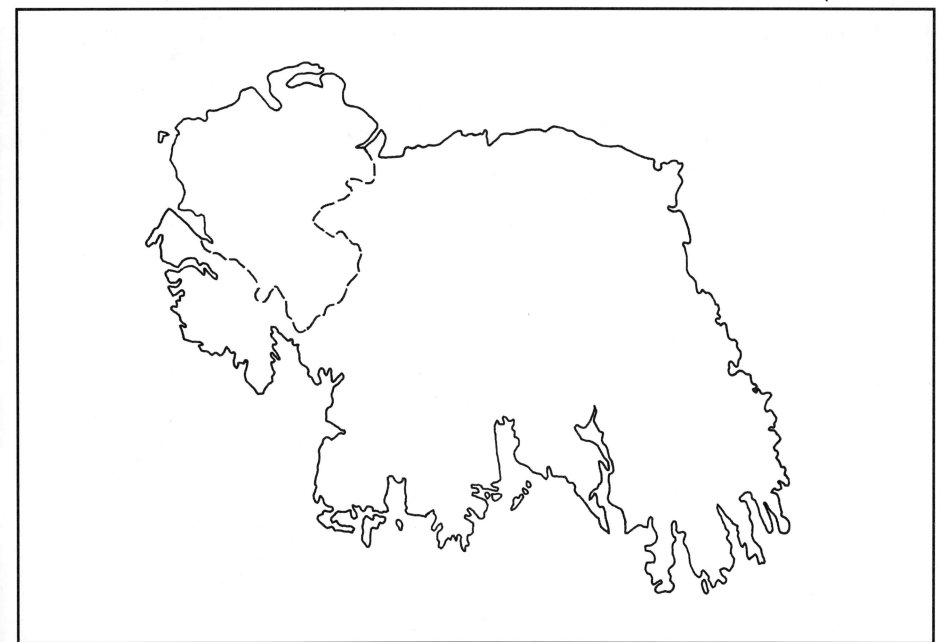

Map of UK

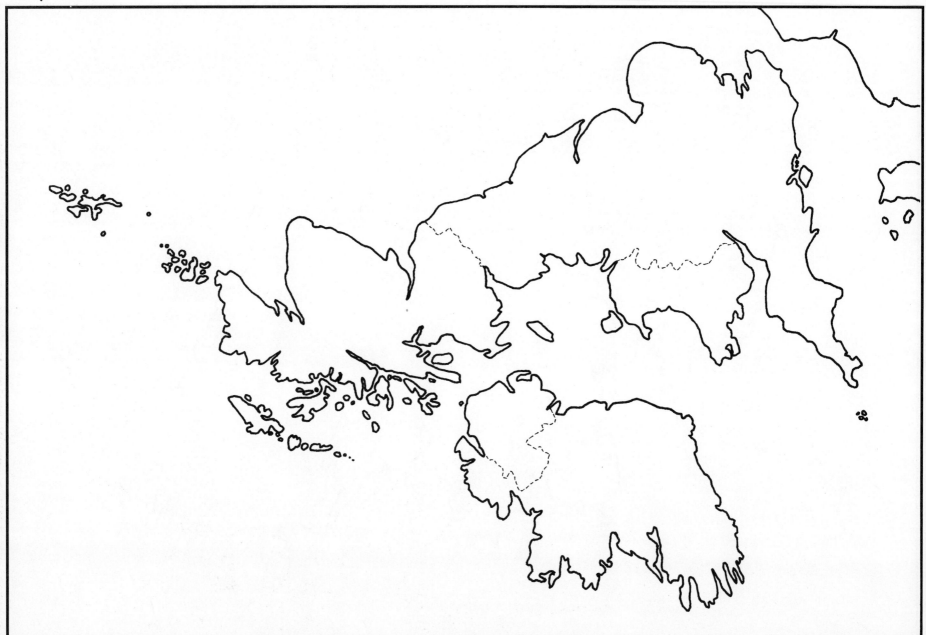

Map of Europe

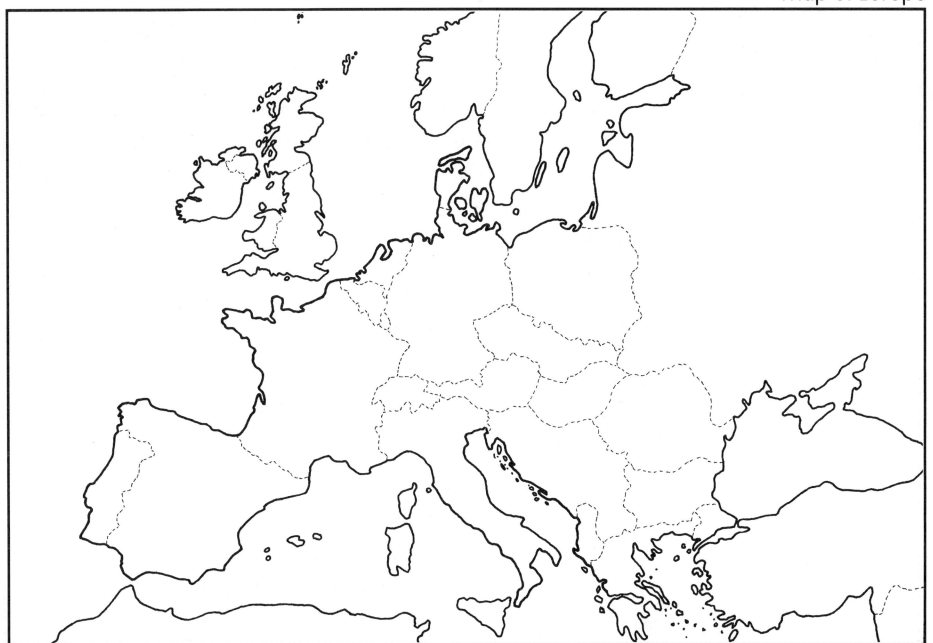

Map of world

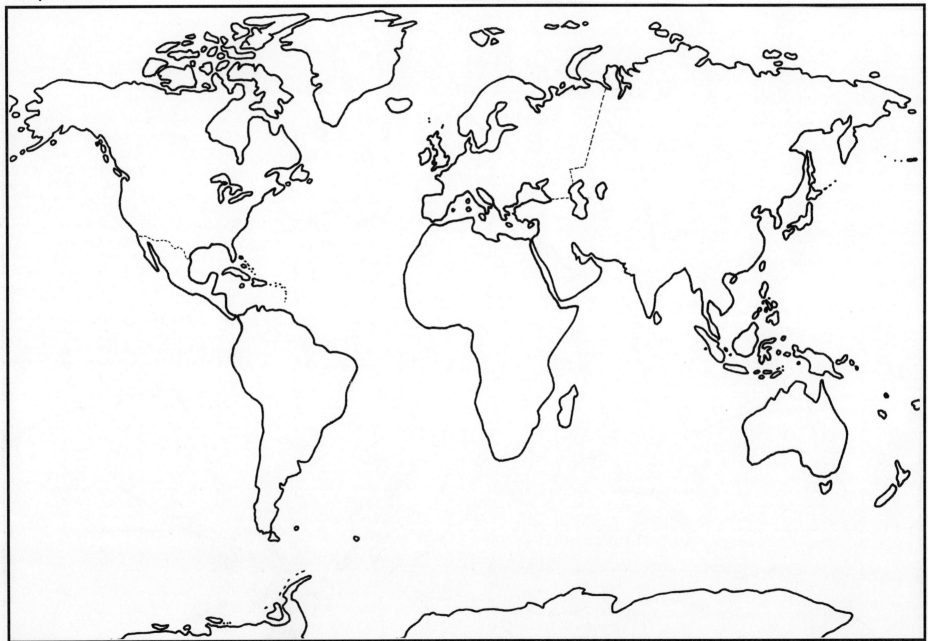

Name _____

W
CROSS
O
R
D
S

Write your clues on
a piece of paper.
Try your crossword
on a friend.
Does it work?

B

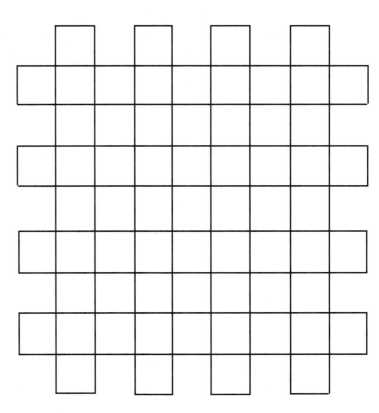

A

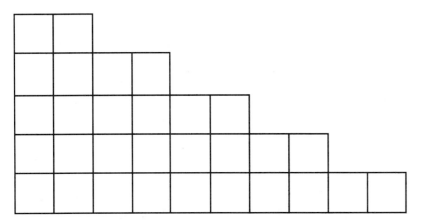

Name _____

Crossword blank 2

The very difficult

W
CROSS
O
R
D

Across

Down

Make up your own crossword. Try it on your friend or teacher.

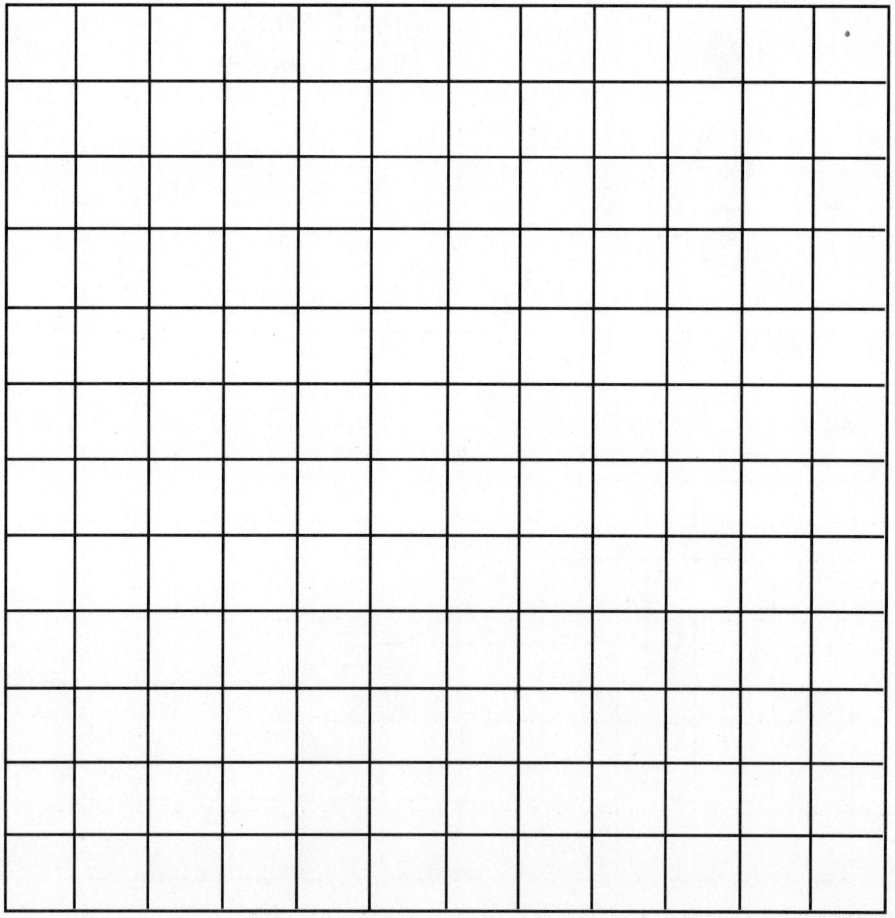

Essentials for every day

Name _____

Wordsearch grid

Picture graph blank

Name _____

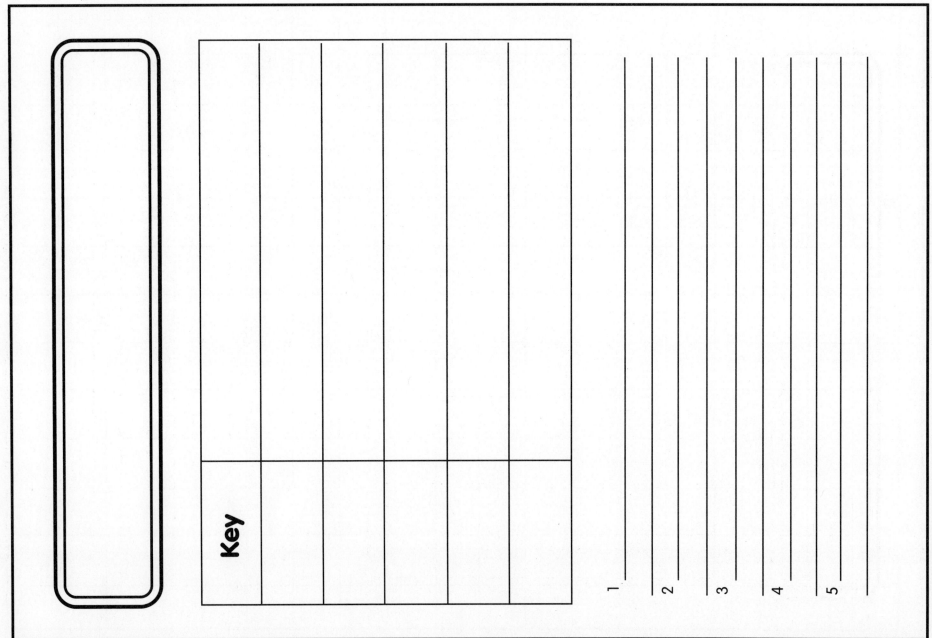

Key

1
2
3
4
5

Name _____

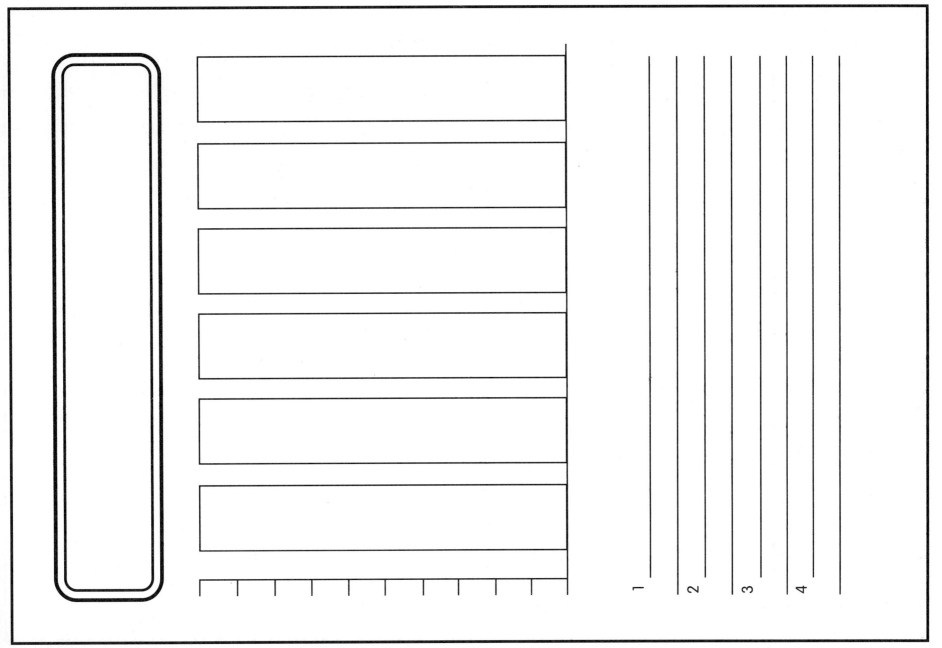

Line graph blank

Name _____

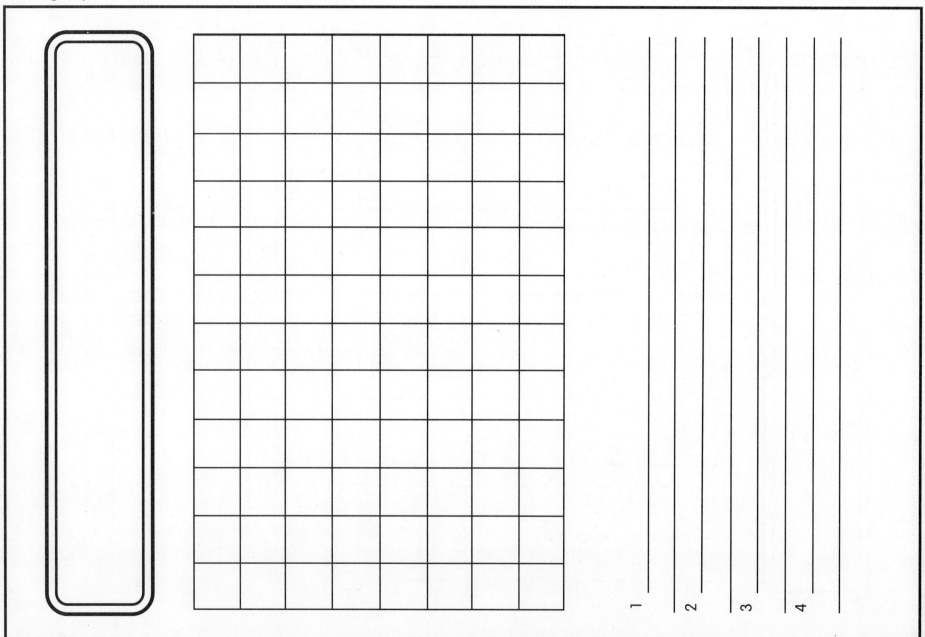

1
2
3
4

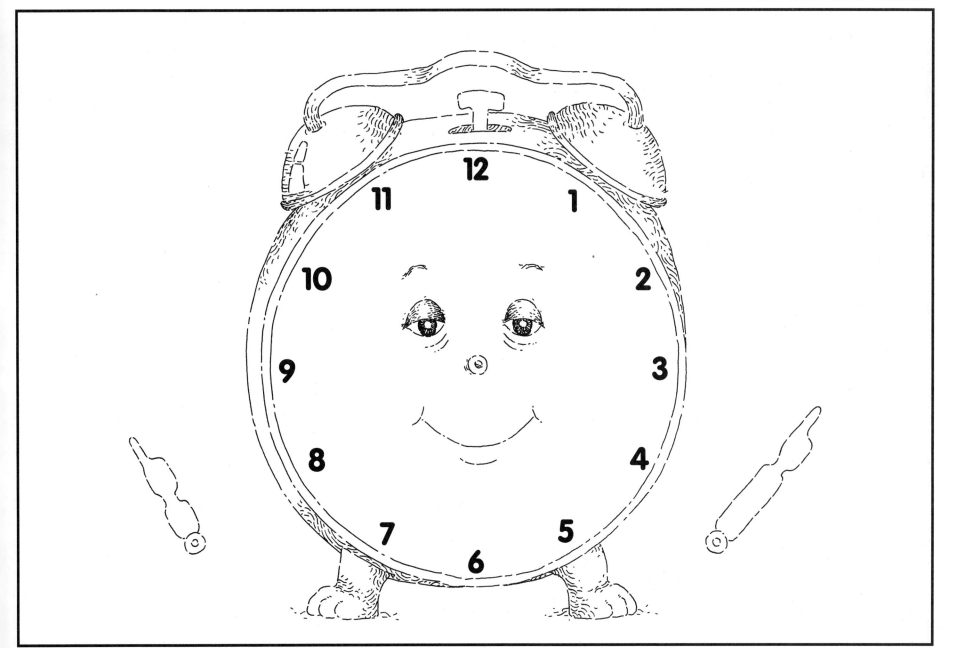

Bookworm head

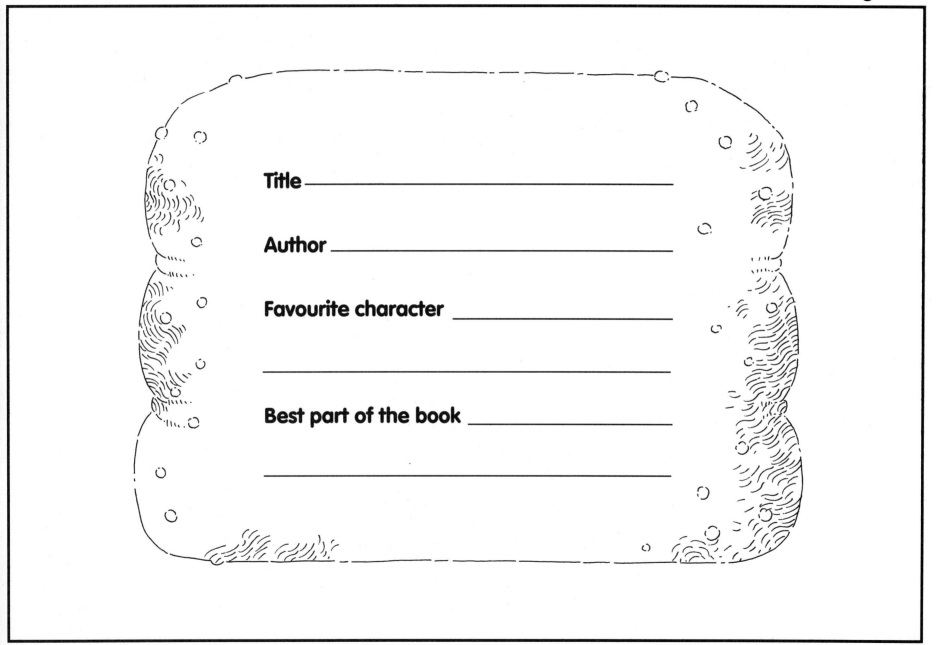

Title —————————————————————

Author —————————————————————

Favourite character —————————————

—————————————————————————

Best part of the book ——————————

—————————————————————————

Dinosaurs

Reptiles

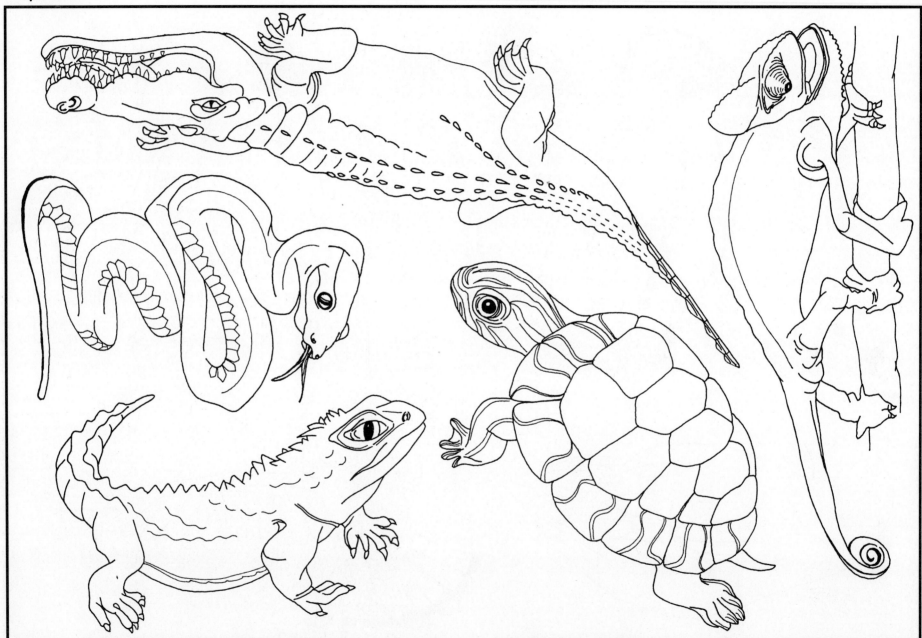

Our Weather

Month _____

Monday	Tuesday	Wednesday	Thursday	Friday	Saturday	Sunday

Weather symbols

Weather chart symbols

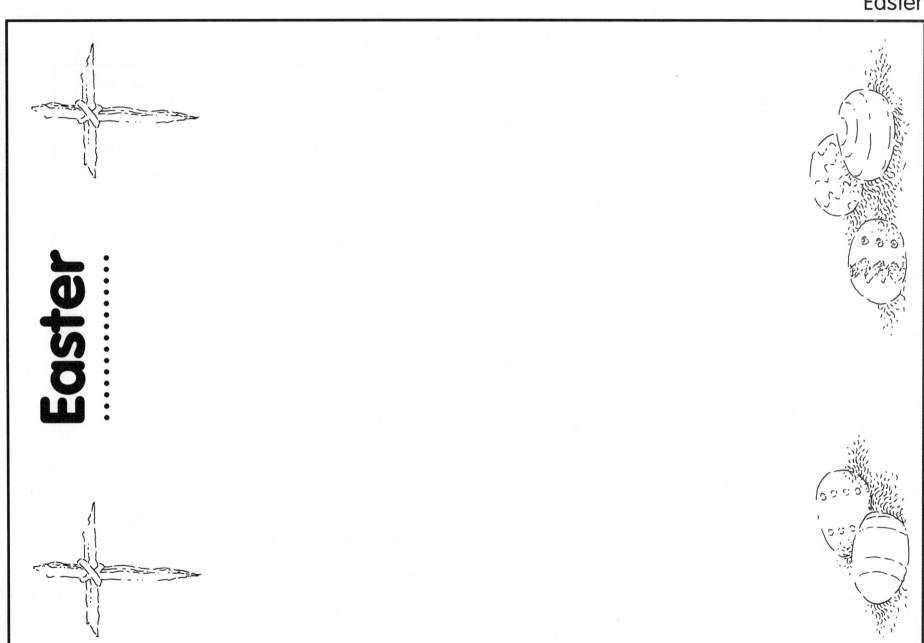

Easter

Christmas

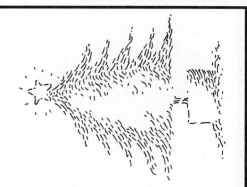

Christmas ••••••••••••••••••••••••••••

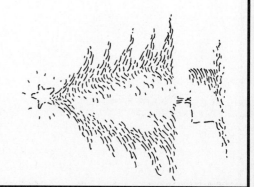

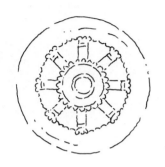

Buddhist Festival

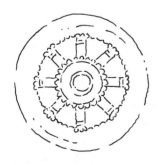

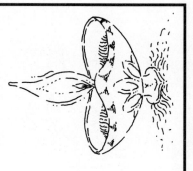

Hindu Festival

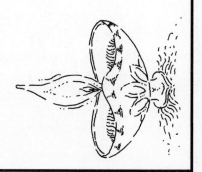

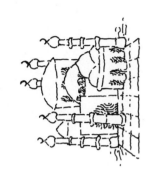

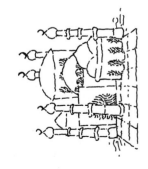

Islamic Festival

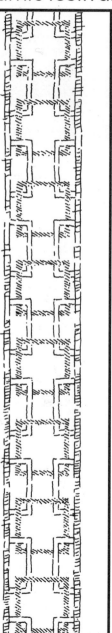

Bonfire night

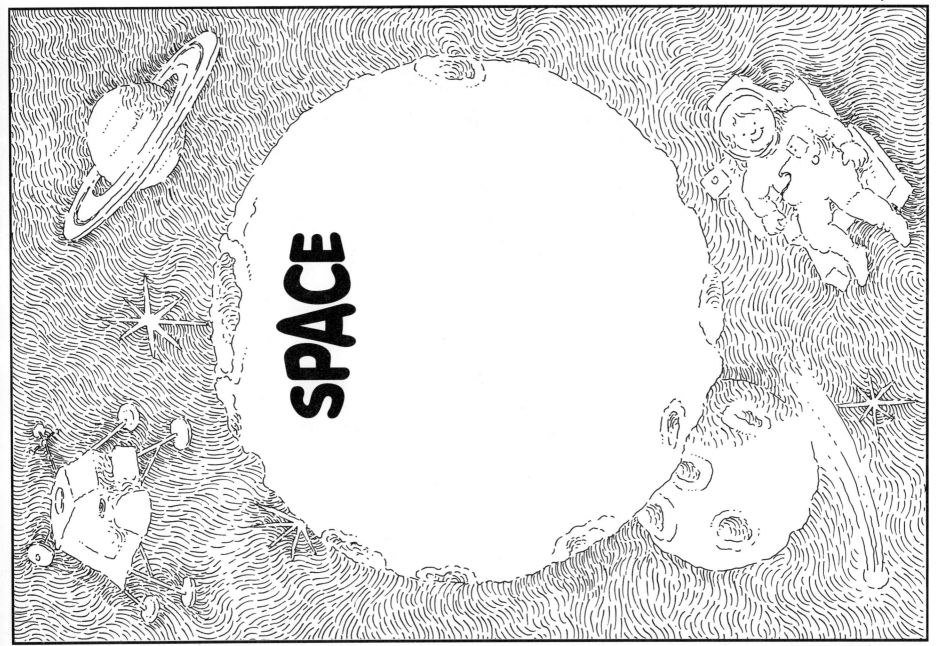

January
February
March
April

May
June
July
August

September

October

November

December

Hope you're feeling better!

Christmas card

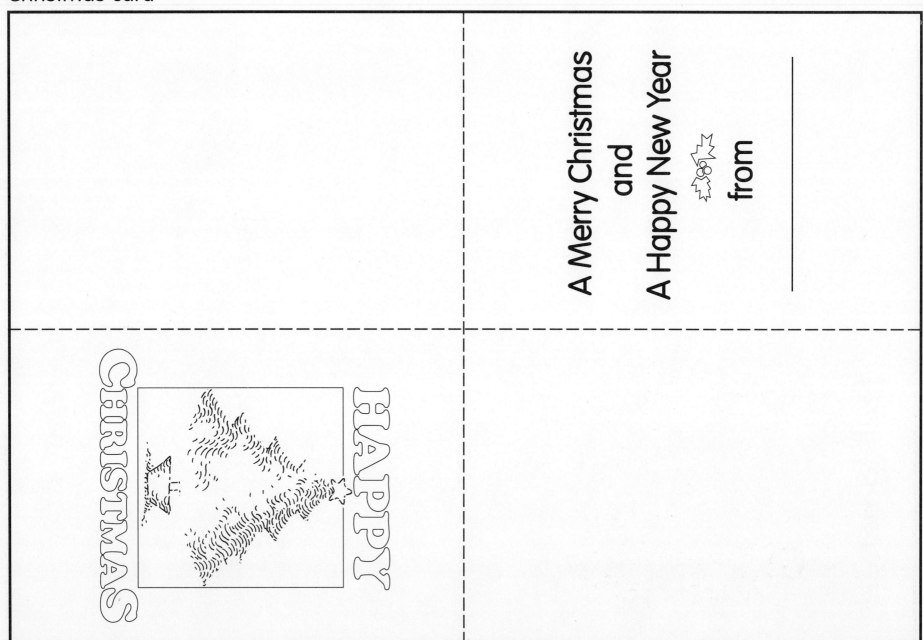

A Merry Christmas
and
A Happy New Year

from

_____

CHRISTMAS

HAPPY

We will miss you

from

_____

Goodbye

Good luck

Name card

Tuck this flap inside

My name is

All about me

Tape here

Name _____

All about me

If I could be anyone in the world I'd be

The most dangerous thing I've done is

One thing nobody knows about me is

The best thing about me is

Lately I learned

All about me All about me All about me

What I'd most like to have is

The best present I ever received is

One goal for the future is

Essentials for every day

121

Name _____

I can

☺ Draw a happy face if you can do it.

☐ Draw a square if you want to learn to do it.

	☺	☐
hop		
skip		
jump		
run		
forward roll		
do cartwheels		
yawn		
wink		
walk a beam		
blow my nose		
swim		

ride a bicycle		
tie my laces		
hammer a nail		
turn on a tap		
use cutlery		
throw a ball		
catch a ball		
do up buttons		
snap fingers		
sing a song		
laugh		
bat a ball		
stand on one leg		
clap my hands		

Essentials for every day

Feelings

   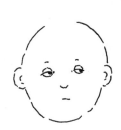  

Draw a face that shows how you feel today.

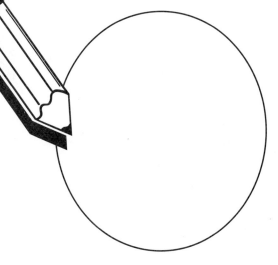

Draw a picture to tell what happened today. Write a sentence about it.

Daily feelings

Name _____

How I feel today

Day_____ Date _____

An important thing that happened today

_____

_____

_____

_____

How I feel today

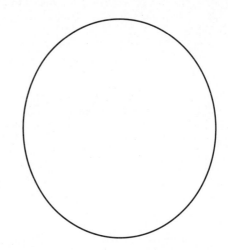

Day_____ Date _____

An important thing that happened today

_____

_____

_____

_____

Name_____

My fingerprints

Right hand

thumb   index   second   third   little

Left hand

thumb   index   second   third   little

Put your fingerprints in the boxes.
Compare them with your friend's prints. How do they differ?
Compare all the prints in your class. Are they the same?

Name _____

Family tree

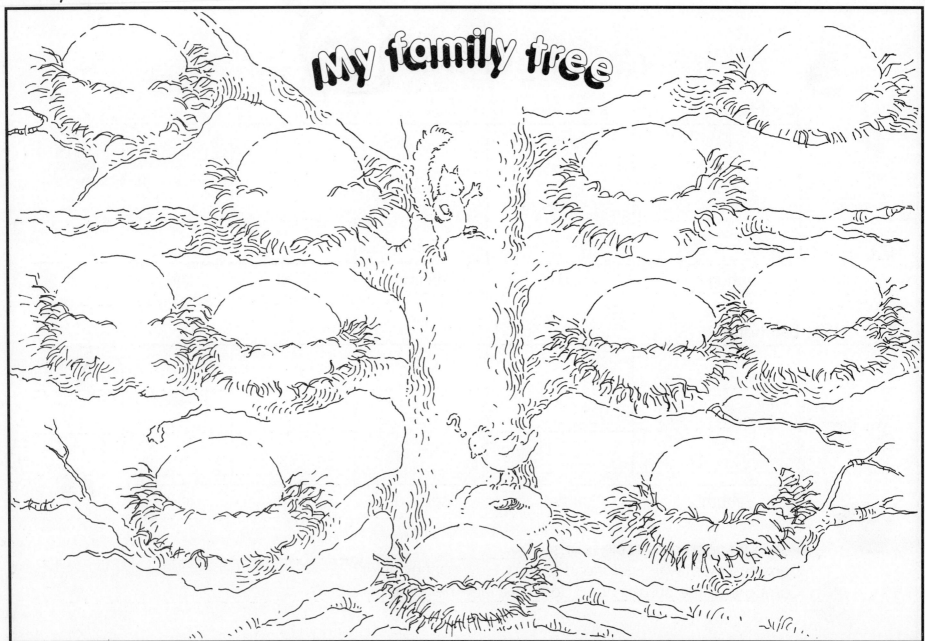

Name _____

My name

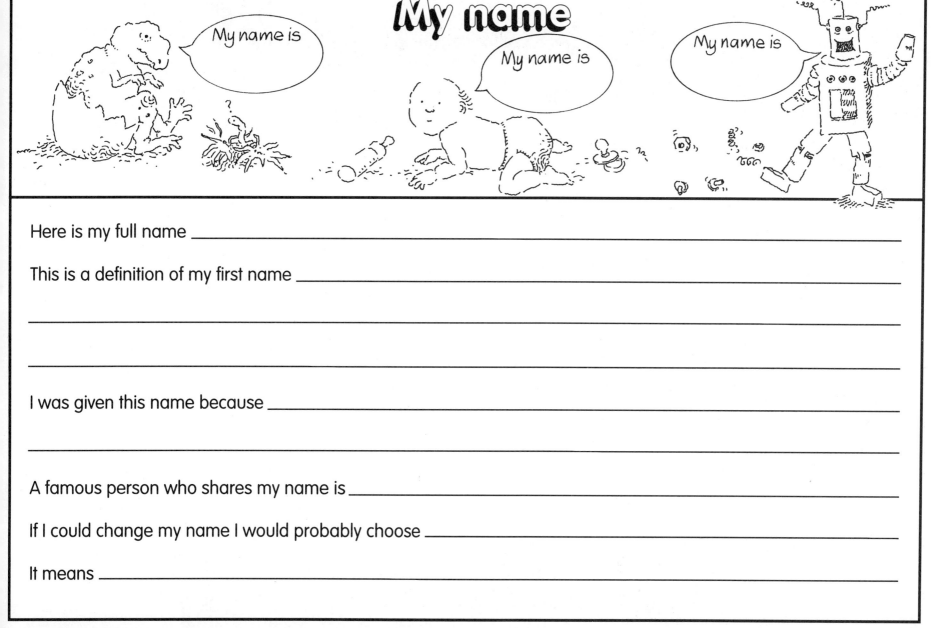

Here is my full name _____

This is a definition of my first name _____

_____

_____

I was given this name because _____

_____

A famous person who shares my name is _____

If I could change my name I would probably choose _____

It means _____

Progress

At the beginning I was able to

Then

Then

Then

My progress

Then

Then

How long does it take?

How well can you estimate?
Guess how long it takes you to do these simple tasks, then time yourself.

	Guess	Actual
Minutes to brush my teeth	_____	_____
Minutes to wash my face	_____	_____
Minutes to get dressed	_____	_____
Minutes to eat breakfast	_____	_____
Minutes to comb hair	_____	_____
Minutes to travel to school	_____	_____
Minutes to say the alphabet	_____	_____
Minutes to read a page of my reading book	_____	_____

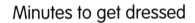

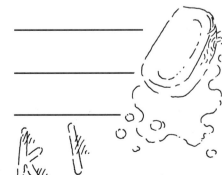

Name _____

Keeping clean

Clean and tidy

It's important to be clean and tidy because _____

_____

My clean and tidy record   Put a ✔ or a tally

	Mon	Tues	Wed	Thurs	Fri
Wash face and hands					
Brush teeth					
Comb hair					
Clean fingernails					
Pick up towels					
Tie or buckle shoes					
Keep socks tidy					
Fasten all buttons/zips					
Pick up clothes					
Make bed					
Keep bedroom tidy					
Help Mum					
Help Dad					
Lay table					
Do washing up					

My health record

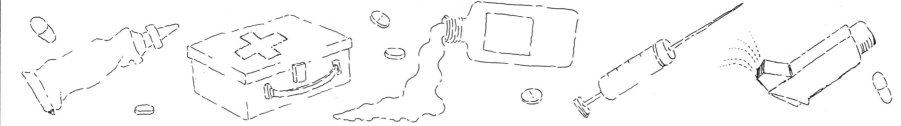

I have had injections to prevent	Date
Diptheria	
Smallpox	
Rubella (German measles)	
Polio	
Whooping cough	
Mumps	
Tetanus	
Typhoid	

These are the illnesses I have had:

_____

_____

_____

_____

_____

_____

_____

Name _____

Size

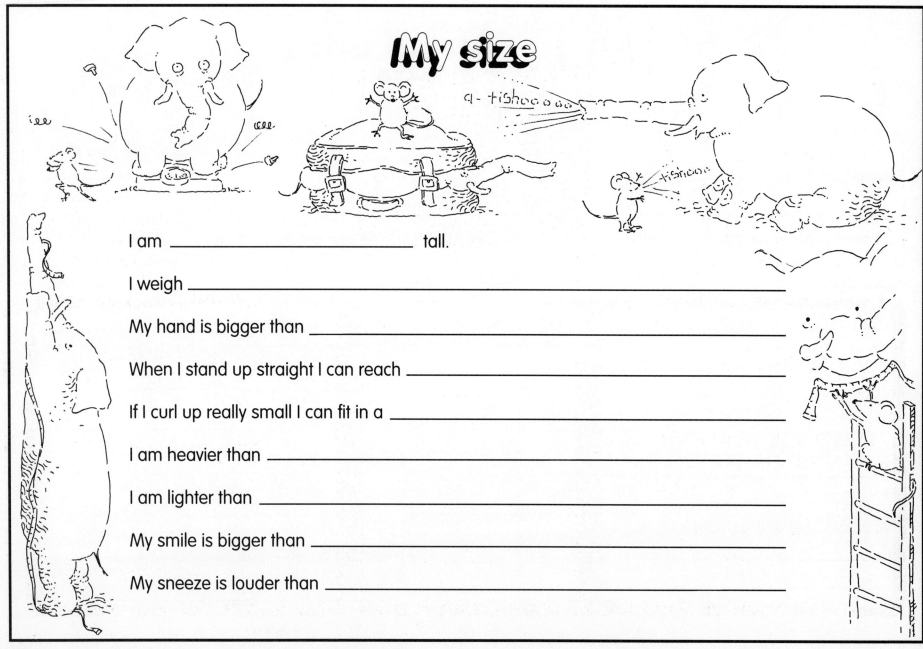

My size

I am _____ tall.

I weigh _____

My hand is bigger than _____

When I stand up straight I can reach _____

If I curl up really small I can fit in a _____

I am heavier than _____

I am lighter than _____

My smile is bigger than _____

My sneeze is louder than _____

Name _____

Make up your own code and try it out on your friend using the names in the computer.

Secret codes

Below are some of the first names of children in this school. They are written in code.

Using the formula A + 2, put their surnames in code too.

Write a letter to your friend who is sick in hospital. Tell him what you've been doing but write it in code!

Below are some unusual
6 19 14 18 6 17 24!
Use the A = 6 formula to find out what they are.

18 20 19 12 20 20 24 10 and
2 14 17 9 10 7 10 10 24 25
_____
_____
_____

Names: _____
_____
_____
_____
_____
_____
_____
_____
_____

The names of some famous people are written below in DPEF (CODE). Break the DPEF and discover their OBNFT (NAMES).

GMPSFODF OJHIUJOHBMF

NJDIBFM KBDLTPO
_____
_____
_____

Name _____

Snakes and ladders

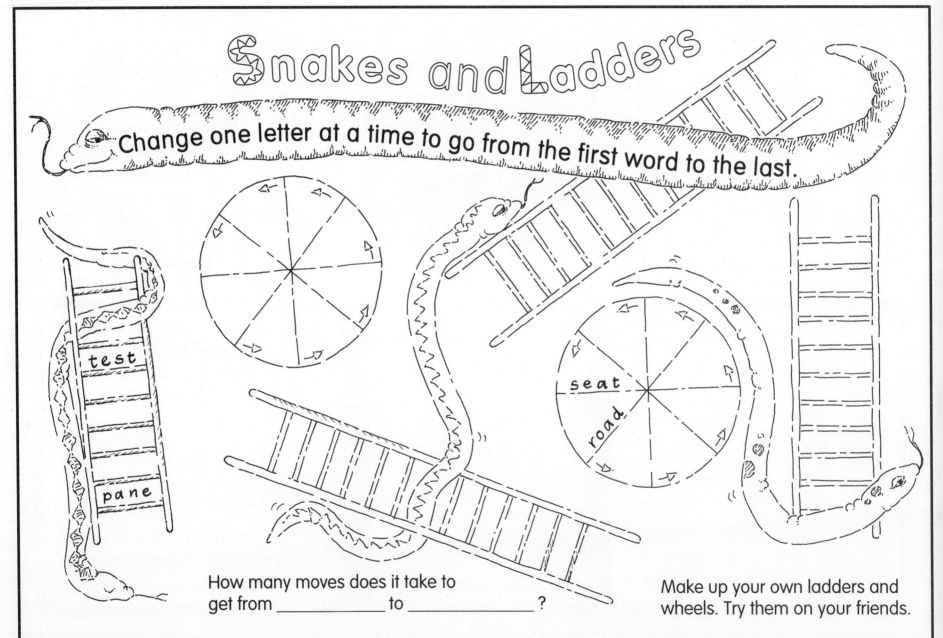

Snakes and Ladders

Change one letter at a time to go from the first word to the last.

test

pane

seat

road

How many moves does it take to
get from _____ to _____ ?

Make up your own ladders and
wheels. Try them on your friends.

Look it Up

Turn to page ___ of your dictionary.
○ How many words are defined?
○ How many definitions for _____ ?
○ Which word means _____ ?

_____

_____

_____

Say it

○ How is _____ pronounced ?
○ What word rhymes with _____ ?
○ Which words have 3 syllables? Write them below.

_____

_____

_____

Choose 6 words and make up a sentence for each one. Write them on the back of this sheet.

Name _____

Let's describe

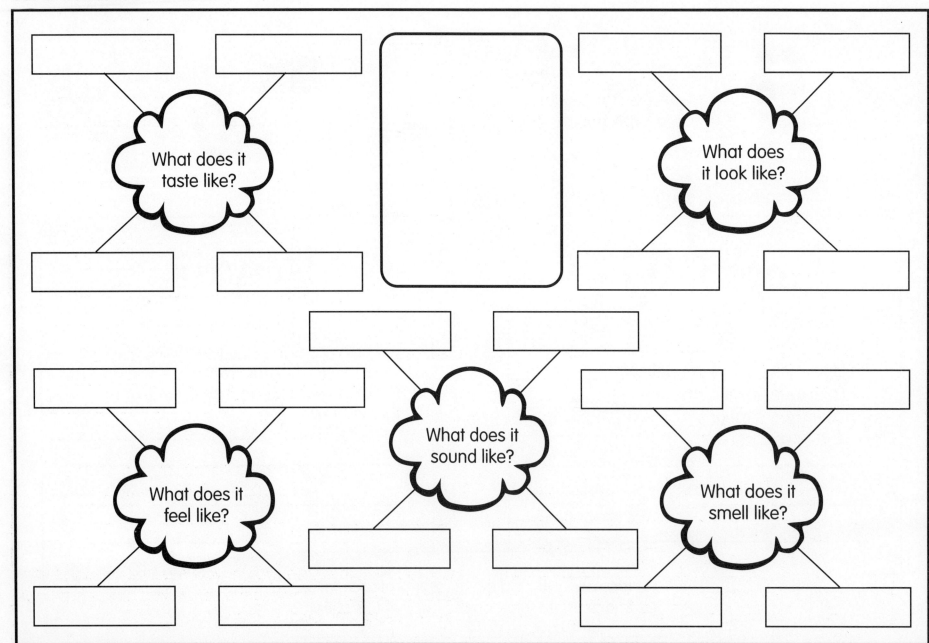

Name _____

Adjectives

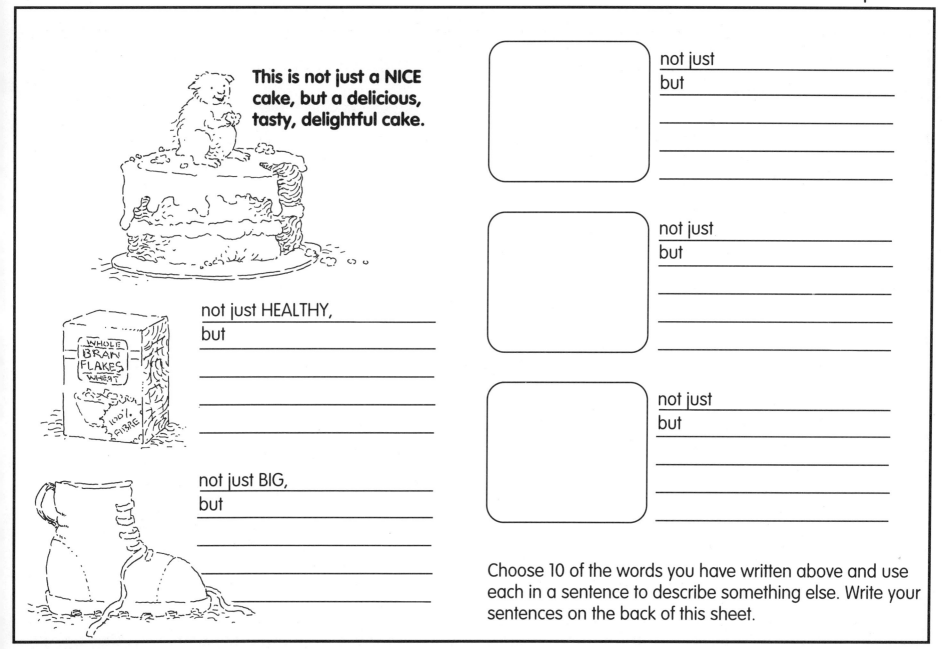

This is not just a NICE cake, but a delicious, tasty, delightful cake.

not just _____
but _____

not just HEALTHY, _____
but _____
_____
_____

not just BIG, _____
but _____
_____
_____

not just _____
but _____
_____
_____

not just _____
but _____
_____
_____

Choose 10 of the words you have written above and use each in a sentence to describe something else. Write your sentences on the back of this sheet.

My set of ...

Name _____

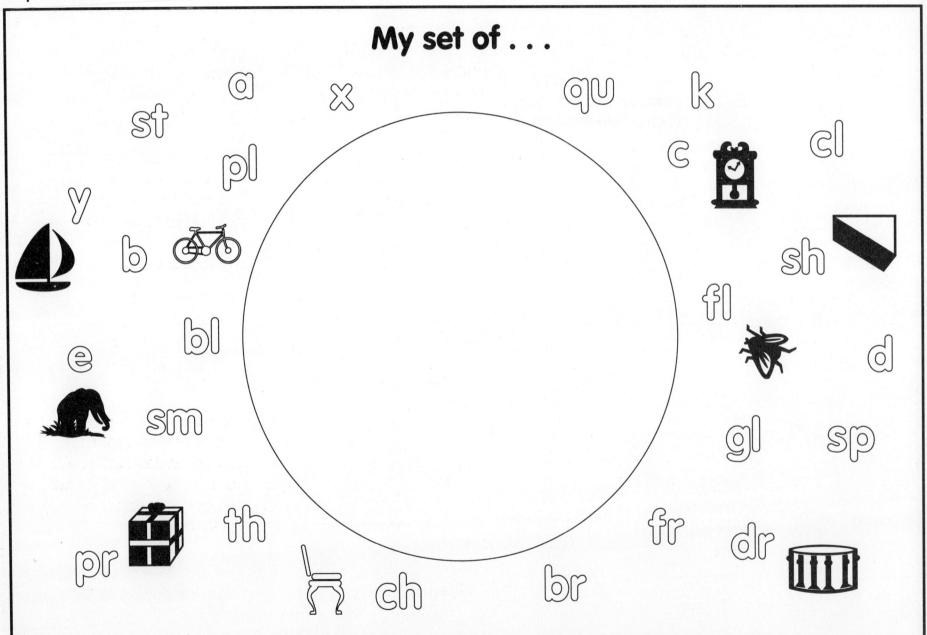

My set of . . .

a   x   qu   k

st   c   cl

pl   sh

y   b   fl   d

bl   e

sm   gl   sp

pr   th   fr   dr

ch   br

Safety first

Make a list of words and meanings which relate to safety and fire prevention.

Find out where your local fire station is. Draw a map showing how the firemen would get to your school.

How often do you have a fire drill at school? How often should you have one? Where are the fire extinguishers?

Draw a map of the school showing exits and doorways to be used in case of fire.

Safety first

Design posters to show what happens when people ignore safety rules.

Discuss and draw up a list of safety rules with classmates.

Find out about different types of fires. What equipment should you use for each one? Make posters to explain the differences.

Name _____

Measuring

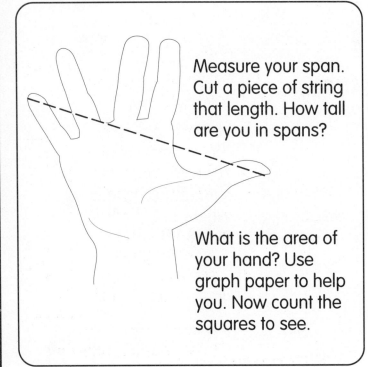

Measure your span. Cut a piece of string that length. How tall are you in spans?

What is the area of your hand? Use graph paper to help you. Now count the squares to see.

How many peanuts will it take to fill a

_____?

Guess and then try it. How far out were you?

Measurement

Use your ruler to answer these!
1 Which is 1mm thick?
a
b
2 Which is 1cm wide?
a
b
c
3 Which is 300mm tall?
a
b
4 Which is 1m wide?
a
b

1 Guess how long each line is (in centimetres).
2 Measure them and see if you were right. How did you measure them ?

Now make up some questions of your own and try them out on your friend or teacher.

Name _____

Listen for 3 minutes.
1 Make a list of all the different sounds that you hear.
2 Are they loud or soft, high or low?

Touch the front of your throat while you sing or talk. What can you feel? Find out and explain what is happening. What else helps you make sounds?

Get 4 milk bottles. Fill each with different levels of water including empty and full. Blow across the top of each one. What kind of sound do you hear as you go from empty to full?

Stretch rubber bands between two nails. Vary the distance between the nails. Pull on each rubber band and let go. Which ones make high sounds? Which ones make low sounds?

Hum a tune with your mouth closed. Now pinch your nose. What happens? Find out why and explain it.

Design and make your own musical instrument. What materials did you use? Make up a piece of music on it and record it.

Square-based pyramid

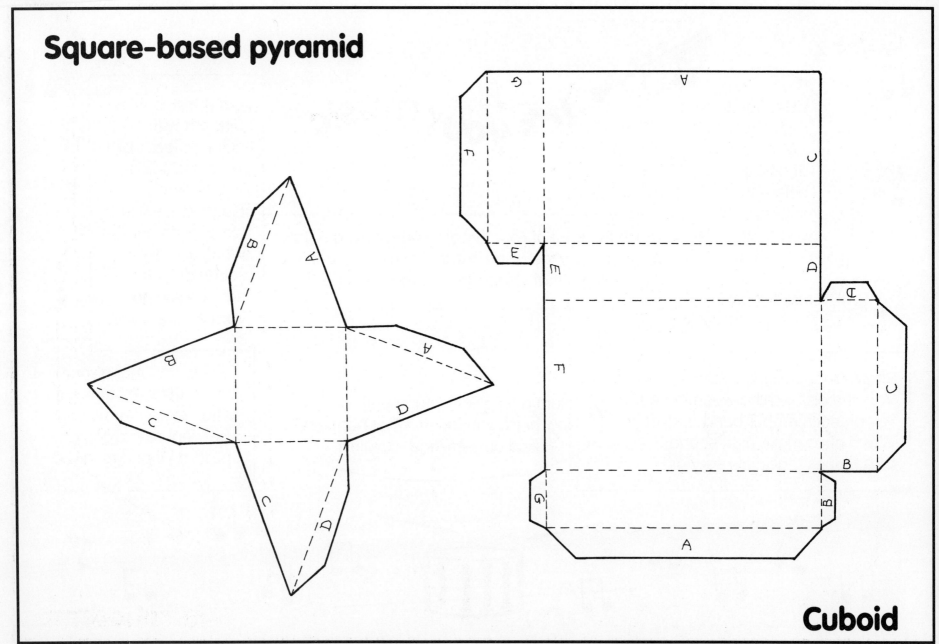

Cuboid

Cube

Tetrahedron

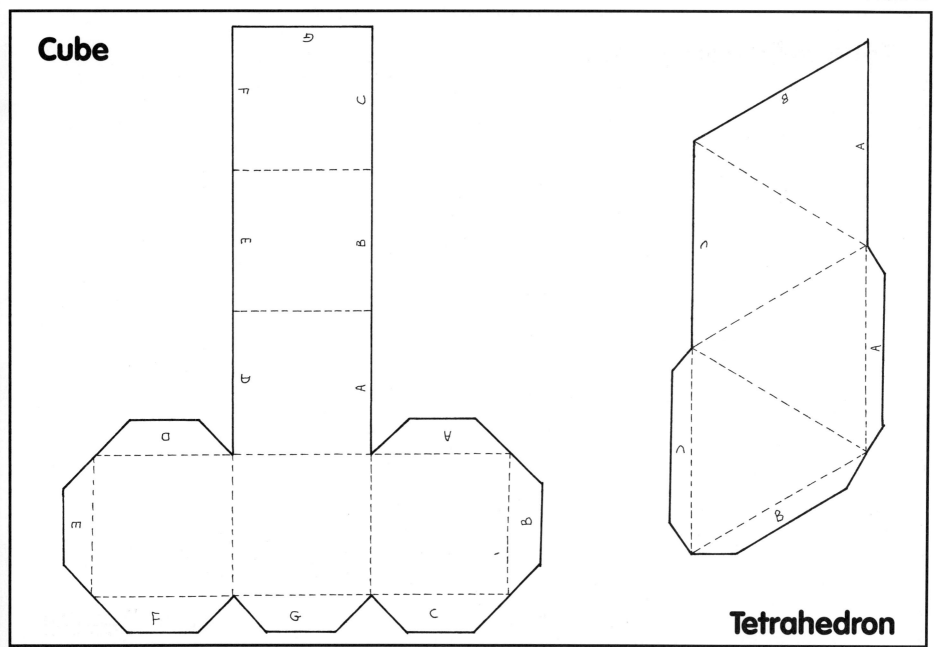

Nets 3

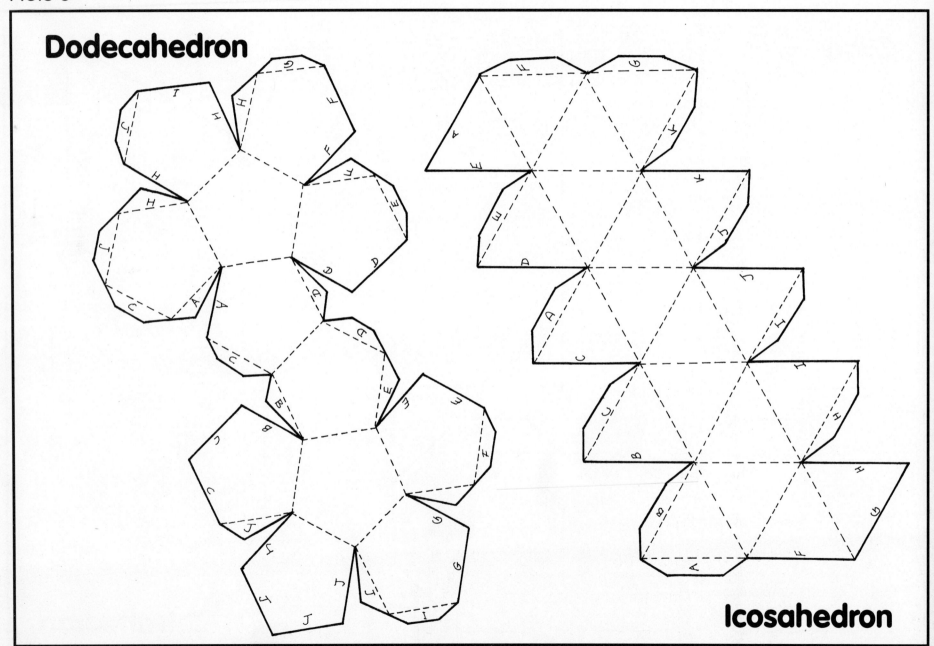

Dodecahedron

Icosahedron